Grades 5–8

Question of the Week

Catherine Valentino

DALE SEYMOUR PUBLICATIONS

Illustrations: Grace Cardoso, Rachel Gage, Carol Verbeeck
Cover Art: Julie Peterson

p. 21:   Illustration from *After Man*. Copyright © 1981 Harrow House Editions
             Limited. Reprinted with permission.

pp. 40–41:   From *Danger, Disaster and Horrid Deeds*. Copyright © 1974 by Yankee
             Books. Reprinted with permission.

pp. 80–81:   From "Lightning Tested as New Energy Source," by Charles Hillinger.
             Copyright © 1979, Los Angeles Times. Reprinted by permission.

p. 110:   Adapted from "Geologic Map of Mars" by David Scott and Michael Carr.
             Published by the U.S. Geological Survey.

p. 119:   From "Perpetual Motion Machines," by S. Angrist. Copyright © 1968 by
             Scientific American, Inc. All rights reserved.

Order Number DS09511
ISBN 0-86651-280-2

DALE
SEYMOUR
PUBLICATIONS
P.O. BOX 10888
PALO ALTO, CA 94303

5 6 7 8 9 10 11 12 13-MA-96 95 94 93 92

CONTENTS

PREFACE

Question of the Week is designed to foster the development of science comprehension and basic science thinking skills in grades 5–8. While teachers agree that teaching students to comprehend what they read is the major goal of teaching reading in school, science comprehension is rarely mentioned as the goal of science instruction. Standardized tests administered each year test for reading comprehension. However, in testing students in science we measure factual knowledge. As educators we use terms such as content, concepts, and process skills to describe our goals and objectives for science students. Consequently, our schools do not have a curriculum or materials to develop science comprehension.

What is science comprehension? It is understanding what science is, what all the factual content, concepts, skills, and methods of science mean. It is the structural framework that allows us to organize all of the content and skills into a meaningful whole. Without that overall framework, science class for a student becomes a task of trying to put together a very complicated picture puzzle without the picture. It can be done, but it is hard, tedious, time consuming, and frustrating. Everyone but the most avid puzzle fan is likely to give up. Trying to teach science using just the puzzle pieces can be equally frustrating.

Mounting evidence about a national crisis in science education at the elementary and secondary level attests to this problem. In survey after survey most high school students, including many of our most able, identify science classes as the most dreaded and difficult of all classes. They are identified with hard work. They involve lab activities and reports. There are standard concepts, methodologies, and techniques that students must memorize. For students who really understand what science is (and is not) these less creative, and possibly mundane, parts of science become meaningful, worthwhile activities. For those who do not, science classes become something to endure in order to get a high school diploma or to meet college entrance requirements.

This is a national tragedy. The ideas and skills of science and scientific thinking are life skills. The National Aeronautics and Space Administration currently predicts that at least 70 percent of the students who are in elementary and junior high schools in the 1980's will end up in jobs that do not exist today. As educators we are given the responsibility of providing a meaningful education for students who will live and work in the twenty-first century, orbit the earth in space colonies, or travel to Mars. We have no choice but to teach the one critical skill that is certain to remain with students—the ability to think clearly, logically, and creatively about the new worlds around them. Science class is the most appropriate place to teach these skills.

Beginning in kindergarten we need to challenge students' curiosity about the world, encouraging them to observe carefully, to ask questions, and to solve real world problems in science. As it stands now, elementary science is often little more than reading a science text and memorizing the right answers. Students classify living and non-living things, grow beans with and without light and/or water, memorize the planets in order, write a report on the advantages of simple machines, and make a volcano for a science fair. At the junior high level, recognizing that the incoming students are deficient in the concepts, skills, methods, and processes of science, we panic. We jump right into a formal discourse on scientific method, the nervous system of an earthworm, and the Periodic Table.

As a result, we never stop to "smell the flowers" in elementary and junior high science education. We end up with a population of students that has a very distorted view of science, one that is never corrected unless they are lucky enough to get an exceptional and turned on science teacher, one of us brave or energetic enough to digress briefly from the standard curriculum. We cannot depend on luck to deal with such an important part of a child's education. Students need to understand that it is the questions about the world that make science exciting, not the answers. The answers will probably change. The basic questions in science will not. *Question of the Week* activities will provide you and your class with an opportunity to know, understand, and enjoy some of the fascinating questions in the world of science.

All of these activities have science comprehension as their major objective. They are designed to help students understand that science is a way of asking and answering questions about the world. Science is based on the assumption that things happen for a reason. We can discover the reasons by questioning, observing, measuring, testing, and then drawing logical conclusions from the evidence we gather. Science takes the place of personal opinions, guesses, and superstition.

Hopefully, students who participate in *Question of the Week* activities will have fun as science sleuths. Equally important, they will become curious, questioning, motivated science students.

Catherine Valentino

INTRODUCTION

Question of the Week is a collection of 16 sets of science questions for grades 5–8. There are four units in each of four general science areas: life science, earth science, physical science, and aerospace science. Each unit is a complete "lesson" that consists of a teacher's guide and four student worksheets on blackline masters: the question of the week, a page of alternate questions, a student glossary, and a challenge activity. The units do not have to be used in sequential order. Also available are 16 posters that display each of the main questions. These posters are spiral bound in a calendar-style format with full color photographs and illustrations. You may use the posters alone or with the corresponding worksheets in this book. The *Question of the Week* book itself may be used independently of the posters, but in some instances the posters help clarify the questions and it is recommended they be used with the book.

1. QUESTION OF THE WEEK The question of the week is designed to go beyond the science questions of standard textbooks. It is meant to stimulate students and to increase science comprehension. Students must approach each question as a scientist would: by thinking, doing library research, and forming a hypothesis. The worksheet has a blank space so students can use the sheet for taking notes or writing their final hypothesis.

2. STUDENT GLOSSARY The glossary worksheet contains 10 terms designed to acquaint students with sophisticated scientific terminology that they may encounter or need to use while answering the question of the week or the alternate questions. Present a copy to each student when the unit is introduced. For further vocabulary practice, have your students use the glossary words in meaningful sentences related to the question of the week. A supplementary set of challenge terms, to be used with the challenge activity or for academically talented students, is included at the end of the teacher's guide for each unit.

3. ALTERNATE QUESTIONS This worksheet offers four alternate questions on the same general theme or subject as the question of the week. These questions focus on higher level thinking skills: the hows and whys of science. They often require students to think fluently, flexibly, and to express original ideas. Many of the questions explore areas of scientific inquiry not covered in texts. Some provide a chance for students to use common sense in making testable predictions about a phenomenon.

4. CHALLENGE ACTIVITY The challenge activity worksheet offers a scientific challenge related to the overall theme of the question of the week. This challenge may be an experiment, a research project, or another independent activity. The challenge activity stresses creative and productive thinking skills, basic thinking and reasoning skills, and scientific problem solving. Some of the questions have no answers, at least none that are found readily in science texts or references in most schools, while others have many answers. Designed to meet the needs of gifted students, this page may also be attempted by any highly motivated student.

5. TEACHER'S GUIDE The teacher's guide is located at the beginning of each unit. The guide contains explanations of the question of the week, the alternate questions, and the challenge activity. It also contains the list of challenge terms for use with the challenge activity or for supplementing the unit.

It should be noted that students are not expected to know the answers to the questions. Instead, they are being challenged to discover them by applying the science concepts and research skills that they are learning in their regular science program. Many of the most intriguing questions in science do not have definitive answers; scientists themselves often disagree. Therefore, students should be allowed the freedom to form their own hypotheses, as long as they can support their ideas with convincing evidence and sound facts. The explanations in the teacher's guide are simply guidelines to generate discussion of the questions and help students develop basic thinking skills in science.

6. OTHER SUGGESTIONS FOR USING THIS BOOK "Learning to Think Like a Scientist," a student handout that can be found immediately following this introduction, is provided to facilitate student involvement in the activities. This reproducible article is an introduction to thinking skills in science. You may wish to use it to start a discussion on the nature of science.

Each unit may be used independently of the others. The time allotted for the questions will depend on the class and the number of activities used. One or more of the activities may be assigned as independent science homework or as a classroom diversion on a series of Friday afternoons.

Encourage your students to make their own investigations in science. You might have them create their own "calendar" of posters and questions as an end-of-the-year project.

LEARNING TO THINK LIKE A SCIENTIST

Do animals dream? Why is lightning crooked? What really did happen to the dinosaurs? Like detectives investigating a mystery, scientists constantly observe the world around them and ask questions about what they observe. In fact, science is really just a logical method for asking and answering some of these questions. *Question of the Week* gives you the chance to be science detectives. A question is always the starting point.

Begin with a Question

Let's practice with this question: "If wind on the ocean causes surface waves, why do waves come into shore all around an island?" The first step is to think about the question and form a hypothesis, or trial explanation. Roll it around in your mind and let it collect bits and pieces of information stored there. Get the facts. How much do you know about waves, islands, tides, and ocean currents? At first you might want to form your own hypothesis to explain what you think is happening. You know ocean currents help push seaweed and driftwood into shore. Perhaps ocean waves are also pushed into shore by ocean currents. This hypothesis is just a guess based on some facts you know.

Sometimes you may not know anything about the question. Then you might start right in gathering information without forming a hypothesis. Ask yourself what information would be helpful in learning about the question and then go find it. When you think you have enough information, then form a hypothesis.

Think It Through

But how do you know if your hypothesis is a good, strong, healthy one? Do some research to gather supporting evidence—hard facts that help guarantee your hypothesis is logical and not just your opinion. You can start by looking in the encyclopedia under waves, or ocean currents, or islands. Perhaps others have thought about this question, too, and published evidence or other hypotheses that will help. You can ask someone else who might know. Scientists might do a computer search, asking the computer to list the references for all science articles with the words "islands," "waves," and "currents" in the title.

Suppose you can't find any evidence that makes sense. Another way to gather evidence is to make predictions that

1

follow logically from your hypothesis. Some of the activities in *Question of the Week* give you a chance to test your skill at making scientific predictions. In this case, you might predict "If currents force waves into shore all around an island, then islands without surrounding currents should have different wave patterns." Maybe waves would even flow away from shore on these islands. Back to the encyclopedia! Or hop a plane to an exotic island to make observations and gather evidence in person.

Design a Test

Sometimes your predictions are best tested by an experiment. In a science experiment you can design a clever situation where your prediction should work. Scientists have agreed on some procedures that are important in planning meaningful experiments. First, your prediction must be carefully worded. Each term must be defined exactly. This will allow you to be more exact in observing and measuring changes in your experiment. Then you must list and describe completely any special methods and materials you will use. Include the number and description of any human or animal subjects in the experiment. Next, write an outline of your procedures exactly as you plan to do them. This step allows others to repeat the experiment and to decide for themselves if your prediction was right. Then comes the experiment. You must keep accurate records of all observations and measurements. You will need these records for the final step, the one scientists and detectives look forward to most—drawing conclusions.

Do an Experiment

Now, how could you do an experiment to test your prediction about currents causing waves to break all around an island? First make sure the prediction is carefully worded: If ocean currents cause waves to break on shore, then islands without nearby currents will not have breaking waves. Next define all important terms such as *breaking waves*, *nearby*, *currents*, and *shoreline*. Make a plan or design for the experiment. For example, a great design might be to observe and measure the exact number, speed, and direction of waves breaking on an island. Then measure the number, speed, and direction of currents around the island. Finally, turn the current off and observe and measure the results. If currents really do cause breaking waves, then you would predict that such waves would disappear when the current was turned off.

The problem with great experiments is they often have a hitch. How are you going to turn off ocean currents? If you are clever, you might figure out a way around this problem. Scientists try to do experiments where they can control all of the things that happen. (Often they put an extra step in the design called a control, just to be sure they understand what is really happening.) Maybe you can do an experiment with a model island and ocean. A rock in the middle of a pool of water and a hose for creating currents might do the job. Then you could measure what happens when you turn the hose on and off.

Make Some Sense of It

The final step is to study the experimental evidence (called data) that you have gathered and to make some sense of it. What is your conclusion? If your prediction was right, you have some data to show that currents cause breaking waves. However, just because your prediction was right doesn't mean your hypothesis is correct. Rocks in swimming pools may not act at all like islands in the ocean. Water from a hose may be completely different than an ocean current. In these cases, it is time to think it through again—with a new hypothesis, another logical prediction, a different experiment, more data collection, and a new or revised conclusion.

Now you are on your own. As you begin your detective work in *Question of the Week*, consider this message from a great scientist and superior thinker, Albert Einstein: "The whole of science is nothing more than a refinement of everyday thinking." Put another way, learning to think like a scientist is really just polishing the thinking tools you use every day.

1. SCARE TACTICS

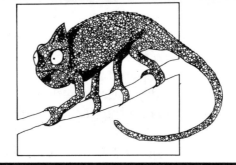

INTRODUCTION

How do scientists use theories to explain different types of animal behavior? In this unit, students are introduced to a general model or theory about animal behavior through specific examples of animal defense mechanisms. The alternate questions focus on specific adaptations of animals living in groups, nocturnal and diurnal animals, and the relationship between an animal's habitat and its defense mechanisms. In the challenge activity students will explore both learned and innate components of defensive behavior as they design an experiment to determine whether or not humans' fear of spiders, snakes, and other creatures is learned or inherited.

QUESTION OF THE WEEK

In what situations will animals try to bluff their way out of a fight? Why would this behavior be a better survival skill than running away from a predator?

Explanation

There are several situations in which animals will attempt to bluff their way out of a fight. Animals often display antipredator behaviors when they are cornered and unable to escape, hide or evade a predator, or when they are approached while feeding. These behaviors are also frequently observed when an animal's home or young are in danger. While these actions are clearly effective in saving the lives of individual animals, they are probably most important for the survival of an animal species. If adult animals in danger ran away from predators, they would abandon young animals or their home territory. This would greatly reduce the number of young surviving to reproduce.

Points to Consider

Animals have developed many ways to escape detection and capture by predators. These behaviors may be grouped into four major categories: detecting predators before they are in striking distance, hiding from predators, evading pursuing predators, and repelling predators. Bluffing behaviors such as hissing, inflating the body, and adopting a threatening posture are categorized as attempts to repel a predator. The chameleon in the poster is exhibiting this type of defensive behavior. In this case the "predator" is the photographer who has cornered the chameleon. Other behaviors in this category include vocal warning signals (apes), mimicry (butterflies that resemble the poisonous monarch), and chemical repellents (skunks).

ALTERNATE QUESTIONS

1. How would an animal's habitat determine which defense mechanisms it evolves? How would you expect the defense mechanisms of nocturnal animals to differ from those of diurnal animals?

An animal's habitat is a major factor in determining the type of defense mechanisms that the animal evolves. For example, an animal who lives in the open plains will use different defenses from those of an animal who lives in the woods. The plains offer fewer hiding places than the woods, so larger plains animals such as antelope would depend on detecting their enemies before they approach. Speed and endurance in evading predators are also very useful on the plains. Woodland animals would not need the endurance to evade predators for a great distance in the dense forest. Plains' predators such as leopards are camouflaged to avoid detection by their prey. In the woods, camouflage and hiding are valuable defense mechanisms for animals such as squirrels and deer that must be exposed during the day. Other elements of the habitats that students should consider include seasonal changes and how accessible the habitat is to enemies.

One of the main differences between nocturnal and diurnal animals is vision. Visual threat behaviors such as changes in body color, puffing up, and threatening postures would be ineffective at night. Nocturnal prey, such as mice, would be likely to use hiding in addition to detecting enemies before they approach. Evading predators, an important daytime skill, would also be important at night.

2.   How do the defense mechanisms of animals that live in groups differ from those of animals that do not?

"There is safety in numbers" should be the motto of animals that live in groups. Since it is difficult for a large number of animals to hide from predators, most groups do not rely on hiding or camouflage for protection. Instead, they usually depend on "scouts" and warning signals. The job of the animal scout is to warn others in the group that predators are approaching. Then the group can flee together, making it difficult for a predator to attack a single animal. A variety of warning signals are used. For instance, antelopes lift their tails to announce that a predator has been seen. Beavers use auditory signals, such as slapping a pond, to warn others. A flock of birds will often attack an enemy together. This defense mechanism is called "mobbing."

3.   What kinds of defense mechanisms do humans show when they feel they must defend themselves?

Angry people shout and show facial expressions such as flaring nostrils, narrowed eyes, clenched jaws, and tightened lips. Their shoulders appear "hunched up" and they flex their arms and clench their fists. Scientists have observed these behaviors in people from many cultures. They are therefore considered fixed action patterns. These are patterns of behavior that are inherited. Other behaviors such as shouting specific words like "help," calling the police, or using charms to ward off evil, are cultural defenses. They are not common to all cultures but are learned and passed on from parent to child in social groups.

4.   Some male fish, such as sticklebacks, and birds, such as towhees, will fight with their own images in a mirror or window. Why do you think they do this?

They react to their own images as if they were other males of the same species (called *conspecifics*). They do not seem to be capable of understanding that they are looking at an image of themselves. These animals fight with other conspecifics because they are protecting a territory, a mate, or a nest. This type of agonistic behavior is a natural way to distribute group members out over the entire available habitat so that they will not exhaust local resources of food and nesting places. Animals living in overcrowded conditions are more susceptible to predators and more vulnerable to contagious disease and weather disasters.

CHALLENGE: Along Came a Spider . . .

Being afraid of harmless reptiles and insects would protect people from possible encounters with poisonous species. Children might learn to be afraid of these animals if they are around people who react with fear or distaste to either an animal or a picture of an animal.

Encourage students to look at objects that are feared in other cultures but not in our own. Have them try to determine whether the fear is learned or inherited. For instance, in certain tribes in Africa, people fear cameras. They believe that the camera "steals their souls" when their picture is taken. Students might hypothesize that in this case fear of cameras is learned, since the camera itself poses no threat.

Look for sound reasoning, a complete list and description of any materials or subjects used, definitions of terms, and a carefully written outline in the students' experiments. You might have them compare experiments and check fellow classmates' reasoning.

CHALLENGE TERMS

- **agonistic**   A scientific term describing fighting, hunting, and competitive behavior among animals, including threats, offensive attacks, and defensive fighting.
- **mimicry**   Behaviors and patterns of coloration exhibited by one organism that closely resembles another, usually unrelated, organism. Animals that use mimicry as a defense mechanism usually resemble organisms that are poisonous or distasteful and thus fool cautious predators. (A viceroy butterfly is a *mimic* of the poisonous monarch butterfly.)
- **mobbing**   A defense mechanism in which a group of prey animals bands together to attack and drive away a predator. Several species of birds display this behavior.
- **ophidian**   Relating to or resembling snakes.
- **startle display**   Animal behavior that lets a predator know that it has been detected. Startled antelopes alert the rest of the herd by raising their tails to display a white underside.

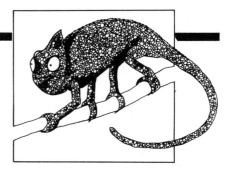

QUESTION OF THE WEEK

In what situations will animals try to bluff their way out of a fight? Why would this behavior be a better survival skill than running away from a predator?

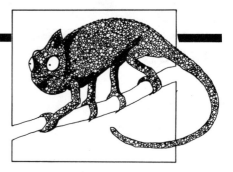

GLOSSARY

adaptations   Changes or adjustments that increase an animal's chances of survival in its own unique habitat. Adaptations can be behavioral (flying in birds, digging in moles) or physical (wings and flight muscles in birds, sharp claws for digging in moles).

conspecifics   A zoological term describing behaviors common to all of the members of the same sex in a species. As a noun the term also refers to the animals themselves. (A male gorilla's chest pounding is **conspecific behavior**; two male gorillas are **conspecifics**.)

defense mechanisms   A general term to describe any of a wide variety of antipredator behaviors such as hiding, making threatening gestures, or emitting noxious odors.

diurnal animals   Animals that are active during the daytime.

fixed action patterns   Animal behaviors, such as startle displays, mobbing, and nest building, that are inherited.

habitat   The special place where an animal naturally lives and grows.

innate behaviors   Behaviors, such as defense mechanisms, that are not learned by an organism after birth but are passed from parents to offspring through genes.

nocturnal animals   Animals that sleep during the day and become active after sunset.

predator   An animal that hunts other animals for food.

prey   An animal hunted for food by another animal.

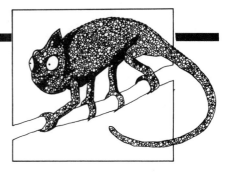

ALTERNATE QUESTIONS

1. How would an animal's habitat determine which defense mechanisms it evolves? How would you expect the defense mechanisms of nocturnal animals to differ from those of diurnal animals?

2. How do the defense mechanisms of animals that live in groups differ from those of animals that do not?

3. What kinds of defense mechanisms do humans show when they feel they must defend themselves?

4. Some male fish, such as sticklebacks, and birds, such as towhees, will fight with their own images in a mirror or window. Why do you think they do this?

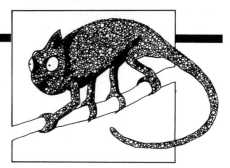

CHALLENGE: Along Came a Spider . . .

Harmless spiders, lizards, and snakes terrify some people without doing anything at all to threaten them. Most people who react with terror at the sight of these animals have a phobia (an intense, illogical fear). Some scientists believe that such fears are fixed action patterns inherited from our ancestors. They think that long ago there were good reasons for this type of behavior. Others think that this behavior is learned by people when they are young. How would these fears have been beneficial to our ancestors? How could a child learn to be afraid of snakes?

Use this information to design an experiment to tell whether such fears are learned or inherited. Make sure you follow the steps outlined in "Learning to Think Like a Scientist."

2. SUSPENDED ANIMATION?

INTRODUCTION

How do scientists use indirect evidence to answer questions about the world? In this unit, students will learn to draw conclusions from indirect evidence when direct evidence is unavailable. Students will explore how scientists use the behavioral and physiological changes in sleeping human beings to draw conclusions about the nature of sleep and dreams in other animals. The alternate questions focus on comparing the specific bodily changes associated with such sleep-like states as comas, hibernation, and the daily pace of three-toed sloths. Designing an experiment to answer the question "Can learning take place during sleep?" completes the unit.

QUESTION OF THE WEEK

Do animals dream? How might a scientist attempt to find out whether a chimpanzee dreams?

Explanation

Evidence gathered in experiments suggests that most, if not all, mammals dream. That is, at regular intervals during sleep, they display the same behavioral and physiological changes that humans show when dreaming. We know about the existence of human dreams from our own shared experiences. We can talk about dreams to others we know. Since we have no way of talking to animals about what happens during sleep, we must see if we can observe behavioral or physiological changes that are associated with dreaming in humans. If sleeping animals display the same or similar changes as sleeping human beings, then scientists could conclude that animals probably dream.

Points to Consider

When scientists observe sleeping human beings, they find that in most people there are periods when certain changes occur. These periods can last up to 90 minutes. During these intervals, the eyes begin to move back and forth quickly beneath the eyelids. Scientists call these movements REM for "rapid eye movements." Muscles in the arms and legs become completely relaxed, or flaccid. Hands and feet may twitch or jerk from time to time. Brain waves, which are measured by an electroencephalograph, increase in frequency. If people wake up or are awakened during these periods, they report that they were dreaming. Most people experience about five regular periods of dream sleep every night. When scientists study animals during sleep, they observe most, or all, of these changes. Based on these experiments, scientists do believe that animals dream.

ALTERNATE QUESTIONS

1. Hibernation in animals is often mistakenly called a deep sleep. How would a scientist tell the difference between the two states? What is the difference?

The scientist would try to discover whether the physiological patterns of deep sleep are the same as those of hibernation. When an animal is hibernating, its rate of metabolism (the rate at which the body burns fuel and uses energy) is greatly reduced. The body temperature of the animal may drop close to 32°F (0°C). While the heart normally slows somewhat during sleep, a hibernating animal's heart rate drops dramatically. Squirrels are true hibernators because they exhibit all of these conditions. However, bears are not hibernators. A bear's body temperature remains near normal, and its heart slows only slightly. Some bears, such as black bears, even come out of their caves in the winter.

2. How is a coma different from sleep in human beings?

Sleep is an active process. It is part of a normal and natural rhythm that is regulated by our brain's biological clock. We can observe and measure a variety of regular physiological activities and changes during sleep. These include muscle activity, brain waves, and REM (rapid eye movement) sleep. A coma, however, is a condition that occurs when the brain is damaged. It can no longer activate sleep/wake cycles. There are no regular physiological changes similar to those seen in sleep. Brain waves are often weak and slow. Eventually comatose people curl up into a fetal position. Their muscles shrink and they lose weight since they are unable to exercise or eat normally.

3. Some animals, such as the three-toed sloth, seem to live each day in a state of suspended animation. Three-toed sloths are nocturnal animals that spend 18–20 hours each day hanging by their claws asleep in trees. They can barely move on the ground and must pull themselves along with their claws. How would such a leisurely pace be adaptive for a sloth? Wouldn't such a large animal have difficulty escaping predators and obtaining enough food? How has the sloth dealt with these problems?

The three-toed sloth has one of the most unusual circadian rhythms (24-hour cycle of life processes such as waking, sleeping, and eating) in the animal kingdom. The fact that the sloth spends so much time asleep is actually an adaptation that protects it from predators. During the day, the sloth is camouflaged among the leaves of trees as it hangs with its feet together and its head tucked against its chest. At night, it spends a few hours

moving slowly along branches eating leaves, stems, and fruit. A sloth's stomach constitutes about 30 percent of its body weight, and it is constantly filled. Digesting a meal can take as long as a week. A sloth is at risk from predators during the few times each month when it must descend to the foot of its tree to excrete unused food.

4. Cryonic suspension is a state in which a body is frozen immediately after death and, in theory, remains frozen until a cure for the cause of death is discovered. Supporters of cryonic suspension suggest that the body could then be thawed, reanimated, and restored to health. In spite of the debate about cryonic suspension, at least 32 Americans have paid to be preserved in a frozen state after death. Others are considering cryotherapy, in which terminally ill patients are put into a cold "sleep" before death occurs. In cryotherapy the patient is not frozen, but is maintained at a temperature close to 38°F (3°C), the body temperature of hibernating animals.

As a scientist, what advice would you have for someone considering cryonic suspension or cryotherapy? What changes in the world would occur if it really were possible to restore a person to health through such processes? What new problems might people have to solve? Would you choose cryonic suspension or cryotherapy?

Most scientists agree that it is impossible to freeze a person for long periods of time without destroying body cells. Thus, even if the cause of death could be treated, there would be no possibility of earthly life after freezing.

Some people argue that even if such cell restoration becomes possible through cryotherapy, it would require perfectly suspended subjects that had not been subjected to fluctuations in temperature. The task of providing refrigerators to house and maintain these people would consume a great deal of space. Large amounts of energy would be needed to ensure a constant low temperature since changes would cause damage to the cells. The chance of damage to the brain and the rest of the central nervous system would be great.

Students should consider technological, medical, and social issues as they respond to this question. Some points to consider are: Cryonic suspension would substantially increase the earth's problems with overpopulation. If space were limited, a society would have to choose whom to preserve. How would people decide? Persons restored to health at some time in the distant future might face psychological and social problems from changes in the world and society. For example, if children were preserved in such a fashion, they would have to face the future as orphans.

CHALLENGE:　Sound Asleep?

Experimental designs will vary, but they should include the steps described in the handout "Learning to Think Like a Scientist." Students should form hypotheses, make logical predictions, and design experiments to test and confirm their predictions. The methods, materials, and procedures should include a description of any equipment, the subjects, their sex and ages, and the steps involved in carrying out the experiment.

One experiment to test whether people learn in their sleep involves presenting new information to sleeping subjects by means of a tape recorder. The information presented is a series of paired English words such as boy-snow, tree-paper, ice-grass. Subjects are then tested to see how many of these pairs they can match while awake. The scientific reasoning for the experiment is as follows: Sleeping people appear to be unaware of events taking place around them. Learning new information takes place when a person receives and processes material to be learned. If, when awakened, a person can recall new material presented during sound sleep, then we can say that learning occurs during sleep.

CHALLENGE TERMS

- **aestivate**　To spend the summer in a state of torpor (compare with hibernate).
- **circadian rhythm**　A 24-hour fluctuating cycle in biological activities that characterizes most living things on earth. The sleep cycle is an example of a circadian rhythm.
- **electroencephalograph**　A device for detecting and recording brain waves.
- **flaccid**　Limp; lacking physical vigor.
- **torpor**　A state of decreased awareness, but not unconsciousness, sometimes resulting from stress or shock.

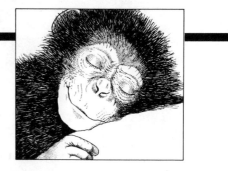

QUESTION OF THE WEEK

Do animals dream? How might a scientist attempt to find out whether a chimpanzee dreams?

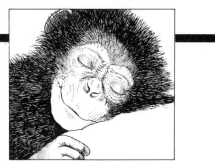

GLOSSARY

biological clock   A biological device, such as a group of brain cells, that regulates the timing of hibernation, sleep, and other rhythmic patterns of behavior.

brain waves   Rhythmic fluctuations in electrical voltage between areas of the brain. When recorded these fluctuations appear as waves.

coma   A state of unconsciousness caused by injury or disease.

cryonic suspension   A state in which a body is frozen immediately after death, and, in theory, remains frozen until a cure is found for the cause of death. Attempts would then be made to revive and cure the frozen body.

dormant   Resting; not active.

hibernation   A dormant state in some animals, such as squirrels, associated with physiological changes such as a lowering of body temperature and metabolic rate.

metabolism   The process by which living organisms produce energy for vital life processes.

physiological changes   Changes in the normal organic processes and behaviors associated with living organisms.

REM sleep   A phase of sleep in which **R**apid **E**ye **M**ovement occurs, indicating that a subject is dreaming.

suspended animation   A temporary suspension of vital life processes.

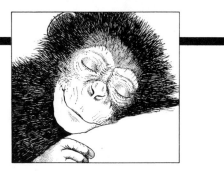

ALTERNATE QUESTIONS

1. Hibernation in animals is often mistakenly called a deep sleep. How would a scientist tell the difference between the two states? What is the difference?

2. How is a coma different from sleep in human beings?

3. Some animals, such as the three-toed sloth, seem to live each day in a state of suspended animation. Three-toed sloths are nocturnal animals that spend 18–20 hours each day hanging by their claws asleep in trees. They can barely move on the ground and must pull themselves along with their claws. How would such a leisurely pace be adaptive for a sloth? Wouldn't such a large animal have difficulty escaping predators and obtaining enough food? How has the sloth dealt with these problems?

4. Cryonic suspension is a state in which a body is frozen immediately after death and, in theory, remains frozen until a cure for the cause of death is discovered. Supporters of cryonic suspension suggest that the body could then be thawed, reanimated, and restored to health. In spite of the debate about cryonic suspension, at least 32 Americans have paid to be preserved in a frozen state after death. Others are considering cryotherapy, in which terminally ill patients are put into a cold sleep before death occurs. In cryotherapy the patient is not frozen but is maintained at a temperature close to 38°F (3°C), the body temperature of hibernating animals.

As a scientist, what advice would you have for someone considering cryonic suspension or cryotherapy? What changes in the world would occur if it really were possible to restore a person to health through such processes? What new problems might people have to solve? Would you choose cryonic suspension or cryotherapy?

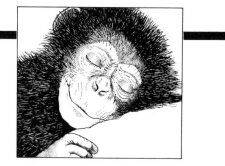

CHALLENGE: Sound Asleep?

Some people believe learning can occur during sleep. They suggest placing a tape recorder that would quietly broadcast the material to be learned next to a sleeping person. Placing a book underneath the pillow has also been recommended. These ideas are especially appealing to students right before a big test. Is there any evidence to support such beliefs? How would a scientist answer that question? What is your hypothesis about learning during sleep? Design an experiment to determine whether learning does or does not occur during sleep.

3. FUTURE FAUNA

INTRODUCTION

How do scientists explain the similarities and differences in present-day animals and those of long ago? Understanding that present life forms are not static, but instead are one stage in a dynamic, unfolding drama of adaptation, is the focus of this unit. Students will learn that scientists use facts and theories to explain present observations and also use them to predict future events. The alternate questions focus on the concepts of natural selection, and how animals adapt to their environment through structural and behavioral changes. Scientific creativity is encouraged as students are challenged to imagine a future in which animals might evolve wheels.

QUESTION OF THE WEEK

What present-day animals might be the ancestors of these curious creatures of the future? How might a night stalker and a flooer evolve from those animals?

Explanation

While answers will vary, encourage students to study the anatomical structures of the animals and to consider the processes of evolution (natural selection and adaptation) before formulating a hypothesis about the animals' ancestors. The night stalker and the flooer are actually bat-like creatures that evolved in the mind of Dougal Dixon, author of *Afterman: A Zoology of the Future.**

Points to Consider

According to Dixon, these animals inhabit earth 50,000,000 years in the future. Human beings and other dominant species are extinct. Conti-

nental drift has shifted the land masses around, changing climates and mixing species of plants and animals. Both animals evolved from bats who flew to newly formed volcanic islands called "Batavia" and settled into all of the ecological niches before other animals arrived. Being free from predators on the island, bats evolved into ground-dwelling creatures through natural selection processes.

The night stalker evolved legs from the bat's powerful wings and developed into a predatory animal whose food supply includes other vertebrates that eventually inhabit the island. Echolocation (using reflected sound waves) is the stalker's only method of locating prey (note the large ears, nose flaps, and absence of eyes). Adaptations such as large incisors and hind legs extending forward below the chin allow the animal to grasp prey.

The flooer has also evolved legs from wings. However, the flooer no longer uses echolocation, but simply waits to snap at insects attracted by its brightly colored ears and nose flaps. The underdeveloped legs are an evolutionary result of the flooer's sedentary life. The color and shape of the ears and nose mimic a tropical flower present on Batavia.

ALTERNATE QUESTIONS

1. What might happen to people if the gravity on earth were slowly reduced to one-half of its present force. How would the decreased gravity affect present-day plants and animals?

While answers will vary, students should base

---

*A highly recommended resource for this lesson. Available from Dale Seymour Publications.

their predictions on scientific facts and concepts. For example, the effect of weightlessness on astronauts in space is to increase the spaces between the vertebrae in the spine. As a result, in the beginning of manned space flights astronauts would complain that their space suits did not fit properly. Once scientists discovered the problem, flexible inserts were added to the suits to account for the growth. If gravity on earth were reduced, students might conclude that people on earth would be taller on the average than they are now. Since less strength would be required to support the body and to do work, muscles would decrease in size. A decrease in gravity would also allow part of the atmosphere to disperse slowly into space. A thinner atmosphere would increase amounts of radiation to which plants and animals are exposed, resulting in an increased chance of cancer. Mutations might develop as a result. Eventually human skin color might darken with increased pigment.

Some plants and animals might become extinct if decreased gravity interfered with seed dispersal or root growth down into the soil. Animals' habitats would be affected by changes in plants. Prey/predator relationships would change. For example, leaping into a tree rather than climbing might be possible for a cat stalking a bird.

2. What characteristics do animals that burrow (including mammals, amphibians, reptiles, and birds) have in common? Draw a burrowing animal of the future, give it a scientific name, and describe its habitat.

While answers will vary, this question focuses on the relationship of body structure to function. Suggest that students analyze body shapes of animals that burrow. Most have elongated, streamlined bodies with short legs. This shape allows them to push through dense earth easily. Their short muscular legs have joints that allow them to "swim" through the dirt. They use their legs as "flippers" to push the dirt behind them. (Some animals that burrow underground, such as worms and some kinds of snakes, have no legs.) Since burrowing animals do not rely on vision

underground, their eyes are small and underdeveloped. However, the sense of touch and smell are highly developed, and structures like paws and noses are often large and elongated. (Note the paws and nose on the mole in the diagram.)

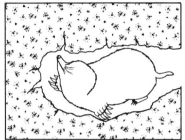

3. Animal vocalizations (sounds) may change drastically in 50,000,000 years. Choose a present-day animal and describe the sounds it makes. Predict how these sounds may change in the animal's descendants.

Answers will vary. Encourage students' predictions that are supported by scientifically accurate information about animal vocalizations. Vocalization in animals has several functions. Changes in vocalization would probably be tied to changes in the function it serves in the animal's habitat. Basically, animals make noise to communicate with other members of their species. The amount of vocalizing depends on the species and its habitat. Animals such as birds and monkeys that live in dark jungles vocalize almost constantly. Their sounds let other members of the species know where they are. They also let others know when predators are around. Vocalizations can mark an animal's territory, giving a "no trespassing" signal to competitors. Animals make sounds in courtship rituals and in situations when they are attacked or are attacking other animals. Bats make high-pitched sounds (echolocation) to locate prey. Young animals make special sounds to communicate messages of hunger and distress to parents.

4. The many kinds of dinosaurs that lived 50,000,000 years ago are extinct today. What animals that were alive at that time have des-

cendants that are alive and easily recognized today? What features might allow an animal to survive over a long period of time? Animals such as sponges, jellyfish, coral, cockroaches, dragonflies, flies, turtles, sea snails, and small mammals were all alive at the same time as the dinosaurs. This list is not exhaustive, and students may name others. Some characteristics that appear to favor survival include:

- an aquatic habitat (many of these surviving animals live in or near the sea)
- primitive body structure
- ample food supply and diverse diet
- large numbers of offspring and few predators
- ability to withstand wide variation in temperature and climate
- small size (this characteristic is closely related to such things as the amount of food necessary to sustain the animal)

CHALLENGE: Going Around on Circles

In order to respond to this challenge, students will need to consider the type of habitat in which wheels would be an advantage to an animal. The following information may be used to stimulate class discussion on the topic.

Wheels are not used universally by human beings as they go about their daily lives. In spite of the fact that roller skates and bicycles have been around for a number of years, why are legs still the preferred mode of transportation? On what types of surfaces do wheels work best?

Wheels are an advantage on hard, flat, smooth surfaces. The softer the surface, the greater the amount of resistance there is to rolling. Heavy objects have a particularly difficult time rolling on soft surfaces. Obstructions like rocks, curbs, rivers, and logs present major problems for wheeled vehicles. The height of an obstacle a vehicle can handle is determined by the size of its wheels. A vehicle cannot surmount an obstacle higher than the radius of its wheels. Hills present a problem for most wheeled vehicles. Cyclists often prefer to walk a bicycle uphill. Very

slippery, icy, or wet surfaces interfere with maneuverability and control of some kinds of wheels. Legs are thus ideal for handling the variety of obstacles encountered in daily life.

Theoretically, if the environment were to change drastically and these obstacles were eliminated, wheeled animals might evolve. Encourage students to describe the future habitat carefully and to identify the types of natural selection pressures that might result in, for example, a roller-skating giraffe, turtle, or rat.

CHALLENGE TERMS

- **continental drift** Slow changes in the relative positions of continents over time. The earth's crust is made up of many sections, called tectonic plates, that are slowly moving and shifting their positions over the outer surface of the earth. The continents were once part of a single land mass formed by several plates which have since drifted apart.
- **Darwin's finches** Several species of finches found on the Galapagos Islands, each of which occupies a different ecological niche. Darwin described these birds and proposed that they evolved from a single species due to the forces of natural selection.
- **The Scopes Trial** The highly publicized trial of a Dayton, Tennessee, high school teacher, John T. Scopes, in July of 1925. He was charged with violating state law by teaching the theory of evolution. Lawyer William Jennings Bryan prosecuted the case and Clarence Darrow valiantly defended it. The judge ruled out any arguments on the validity of Darwin's theory. Scopes was found guilty and fined $100.
- **ubiquitous** Existing or being everywhere at the same time: constantly encountered.
- **vestigial organs** Bodily organs that serve no useful purpose due to evolutionary changes in an animal. The appendix is considered by most zoologists to be a vestigial organ in human beings.

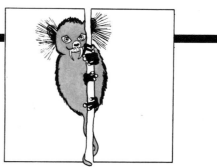

QUESTION OF THE WEEK

What present-day animals might be the ancestors of these curious creatures of the future? How might a night stalker and a flooer evolve from those animals?

Night Stalker   Flooer

GLOSSARY

adaptations   Changes or adjustments that increase an animal's, or a plant's, chances of survival in its own unique habitat. Adaptations can be behavioral or physical.

descendants   Any offspring that derive from an earlier form.

echolocation   A process for locating objects (such as prey) by means of "bouncing" sound waves off of the objects and thus detecting the objects by the echo or returning sound.

ecological niche   The place or position within a plant's or animal's habitat to which it is particularly suited because of its specialized body parts, diet, and behaviors.

evolution   The process in which new species of plants and animals develop from modifications of earlier generations.

extinction   The process in which entire species of plants and animals cease to exist on earth.

fauna   The animals of a particular region, period, or special environment.

flora   The plants of a particular region, period, or special environment.

mutation   A significant and relatively permanent inherited change in plants and animals. Usually the change occurs in the chromosomes or genes.

natural selection   An explanation, first proposed by Darwin, that accounts for the evolution of new species of plants and animals. According to this hypothesis, evolution occurs when the environment changes. If certain genetic traits increase the chances of an individual's survival, then individuals possessing those traits will be more likely to survive and reproduce. Therefore, the traits will be more likely to be passed along to future generations. Eventually the traits will be shared by most individuals in the species.

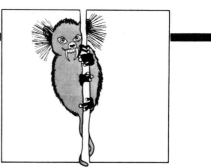

ALTERNATE QUESTIONS

1. What might happen to people if the gravity on earth were slowly reduced to one-half of its present force. How would the decreased gravity affect present-day plants and animals?

2. What characteristics do animals that burrow (including mammals, amphibians, reptiles, and birds) have in common? Draw a burrowing animal of the future, give it a scientific name, and describe its habitat.

3. Animal vocalizations (sounds) may change drastically in 50,000,000 years. Choose a present-day animal and describe the sounds it makes. Predict how these sounds may change in the animal's descendants.

4. The many kinds of dinosaurs that lived 50,000,000 years ago are extinct today. What animals that were alive at that time have descendants that are alive and easily recognized today? What features might allow an animal to survive over a long period of time?

CHALLENGE: Going Around on Circles

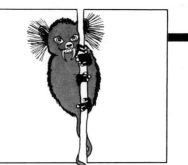

Human beings are constantly designing new and better ways to move quickly and efficiently on land. The invention of the wheel is probably the single greatest achievement towards that goal. The wheel made wagons, carriages, bicycles, and automobiles possible. Each of these machines, in turn, has made it possible for human beings to travel faster and farther using less human energy. Given the advantages of wheels, some scientists have asked the question, "Why haven't animals evolved wheels rather than feet at the end of their legs?" Suppose animals of the future could evolve retractable wheels made of cartilage on the bottom of their feet. In scientific terms, what would be the disadvantages of wheels as a body structure? Imagine the world as it might be 25 million years from now. Some animals have evolved wheels as a means of locomotion. Describe a wheeled animal of the future, and explain the forces that caused the development of wheels in the species.

4. WHAT'S FOR LAUNCH?

Life Science

INTRODUCTION

How do scientists use a theory or model to explain a single observation? In this unit, students must use the theory that any consistently observed behavior in living things, such as ejecting spores in a puffball fungus, has some adaptive value. In order to answer the alternate questions, they must start with the theory that all life forms share common elements and are part of an interrelated life-support cycle. Throughout the unit, students will learn basic ecological concepts. They must apply this knowledge and common sense to create a menacing organism in the challenge activity.

QUESTION OF THE WEEK

How does a puffball fungus eject spores into the air? What triggers this response? Why is this adaptation better for the puffball than dropping spores as many fungi do?

Explanation

In the puffball fungus, the spores are contained in a pod resembling a puffy ball at the top of a long stalk. When the fungus is ready to begin its reproductive cycle, it has a special adaptation that ensures its spores will be distributed to new areas for germination. The stalk first grows up from the forest floor holding the puffball away from competing dense undergrowth such as moss and forest debris. (Note: there are also short-stemmed puffballs that grow in grassy fields and meadows.) As the puffball matures it dries out, leaving a hollow "ball" filled with spores. There it awaits a drop of rain, or an accidental bump from a passing animal or falling twig, to "puff" some of the spores from a small opening in the top of the ball. The wind then carries the

spores, often for hundreds of miles. Puffballs and similar fungi that eject spores into the air occupy different niches from those occupied by mushroom fungi that drop spores from beneath a gilled cap or flat fungi that grow on treetrunks and deposit spores into the air. Unlike these fungi, puffballs can grow in areas of thick undergrowth. However, without a breeze to carry the spores aloft, the puffball would become extinct. The long stalk that carries the spores above the underbrush and the ability to fire spores into a layer of active air are unique adaptations that ensure the survival of the puffball.

Points to Consider

Students will need to use biological "common sense" to respond to this question since most science reference books do not specifically address the question as stated. Draw attention to the mossy undergrowth around the puffball and to the relatively long stemlike structure supporting the spore pod or case. Challenge students to consider why a plant would evolve one method of spore distribution over another. It may be helpful for them to consider various questions about methods of seed distribution. For example, what types of plants scatter many seeds indiscriminately in the wind? (Grasses and weeds that can thrive in most biomes scatter their seeds.) What others have very specific methods of distribution? (Plants that are uniquely adapted to one niche have specific methods of distribution such as certain flowering plants [orchids], conifers [evergreens like the sequoia], and nut trees [the coconut palm].)

ALTERNATE QUESTIONS

1. What would the effect be on human

beings if all of the fungi on earth suddenly disappeared?

Fungi have the major responsibility (along with bacteria) for breaking down organic matter and releasing carbon, oxygen, nitrogen, and phosphorous into the soil and atmosphere. Without fungi, these elements would be trapped forever in the bodies of dead plants and animals. Human beings would eventually face a depletion of life-supporting resources. Dead matter and other organic waste would accumulate, and people would be subjected to disease as bacteria multiplied. The supply of natural fertilizer for farmlands would be eliminated, causing the world's food supply to dwindle. Bread leavened with yeast and certain types of cheese would disappear. Many antibiotics could not be manufactured without fungi, and the diseases cured by these drugs would increase.

2.   In spite of efforts to develop an effective fungicide, the chestnut forests of the United States have been destroyed by the chestnut blight fungus. Dutch elm disease, also caused by a fungus, has destroyed elms in North America and Europe. Ringworm and athlete's foot are common fungal infections in human beings. They are very contagious and difficult to prevent or cure. Rusts and smuts plague farmers. What characteristics of these fungi make them so difficult to control?

Fungi thrive in large numbers almost everywhere on earth. They live in rivers, lakes, and streams; in plants and animals; in the arctic and the tropics. This ability to grow and reproduce in a wide variety of habitats makes them particularily hard to control. The fact that fungi do not produce their own food, but depend on a host plant or animal, is a major problem in producing effective fungicides. It is virtually impossible to eliminate fungi from a forest of chestnut or elm trees without damaging the trees themselves. Since spores are usually dispersed by the wind, they can spread from plant to plant without being detected. Fungi thrive in moist places such as locker room floors or showers, where they spread athlete's foot and other fungal conditions

from person to person. The fact that they are beneficial to human beings precludes using controls that eliminate them entirely on earth. (See alternate question 1.) The fact that spores are too small to be seen easily makes it difficult to spot a fungus infection in its early stages when it is easier to treat.

3.   How are a fertilized chicken egg, a peanut, and a spore alike? How are they different? Describe as many similarities and differences as you can.

Answers will vary. Stimulate fluency, flexibility, and originality of ideas by encouraging students to compare the three objects in as many different ways as they can. They may include insignificant or trivial similarities and differences.

Sample Similarities:
- They are part of a reproductive cycle in a living thing.
- They are comprised of cells.
- They all need food and water in order to develop into mature organisms.
- They increase in size as they grow.
- They can be destroyed by harsh environmental conditions.
- All three can be found in and around most homes in the United States.
- They will eventually die.

Sample Differences:
- A chicken egg and a peanut can be seen with the naked eye while a spore is often too small.
- The chicken egg comes from an animal while the peanut and the spore come from plants.
- The chicken egg and the peanut are part of a cycle of sexual reproduction. Some spores develop sexually while others develop asexually.
- The chicken egg and the peanut are protected by a hard outer shell while the spore is not.
- The spore is usually a single cell while the peanut and chicken egg are comprised of many cells.
- They are different colors, shapes, and sizes.
- A chicken egg will roll while a peanut and a spore will not.

4.   Centuries ago, people who observed

large circles of mushroom growth in fields believed that they marked the paths of dancing fairies. They called them "fairy rings." How would a scientist today explain these rings of fungi?

The fairy ring is caused by the reproductive cycle of certain fungi. The typical fungus consists of a mass of threadlike filaments called *hyphae*. These filaments make up the mycelium, or food-gathering part of the fungus. The mycelium feeds on dead or decaying matter by branching out in a circle just below the surface of the soil. When the mycelium is ready to reproduce, it produces mushrooms that break through the ground in a ring marking the end of the mycelium growth. (The ring of mushrooms is easy to see because the growth of grass inside the ring is inhibited by the underground growth of the mycelium. Outside the ring the grass is often green and lush from nitrogen released by the mycelium.) The mushrooms then release spores from their gills. As these spores germinate they each develop a new mycelium that continues to grow outward in circles underground. When the new mycelium is ready to reproduce, it sends up another ring of mushrooms. It is this series of rings, caused by the reproductive cycle of fungi, that people long ago mistook for fairy rings.

CHALLENGE: Seeing Is Not Believing!

The ratio of an animal's body surface area to its body volume is important in determining how large a land animal on earth can become. For example, even doubling the size of invertebrates, such as beetles and spiders, would increase their weight eight times, while their muscle tissue would be only four times as large. A much thicker exoskeleton and larger muscle system would be needed to make moving and obtaining food possible for such creatures. An internal support system such as the bony skeleton of vertebrates provides the necessary support for large land animals.

In the sea, however, water supports the bodies of animals. Vertebrates such as the blue whale can reach lengths of 110 feet (33.6 m), and invertebrates such as the giant squid can reach lengths of 60 feet (18 m). One of the main limiting factors for sea creatures is food supply. The amount of food needed is proportional to the mass of the animal. If a creature were too large, it would have to spend more than all its time eating, which is clearly impossible.

Some real "monsters" that students might use as characters include the bird-eating spider from South America with a 3.5-inch (8.75-cm) body and a 10-inch (25-cm) leg span; the African giant snail that measures 15.5 inches (38.75 cm) from snout to tail; the giant earthworm from South Africa that can be as large as 22 feet (6.7 m) when fully extended; and the 10-foot (3-m) long Komodo dragon, the world's largest lizard. Monster plants might include seaweed which can reach lengths of 190 feet (58 m); the stinking corpse lily with a blossom 3 feet (0.9 m) in diameter; and the Venus flytrap, which entraps small animals and digests them with chemical secretions.

CHALLENGE TERMS

- **fungus garden**   A name commonly given to growths of fungi cultivated by some termites for food.
- **mycology**   The scientific term for the study of fungi; derived from the Greek word for mushroom, *mykes*.
- **saprobiosis**   The process of getting nutrients from dead organic matter. Fungi are saprobes.
- **sporophore**   The part of a fungus that is generally visible and is the "fruiting" or spore-producing body of the fungus. The largest puffball fungus sporophore on record measured 60 inches (150 cm) in diameter.
- **symbiosis**   A close relationship between two organisms from which both benefit.

QUESTION OF THE WEEK

How does a puffball fungus eject spores into the air? What triggers this response? Why is this adaptation better for the puffball than dropping spores as many fungi do?

GLOSSARY

blight   A disease or injury to plants that interferes with plant growth and causes the plant to yellow, wither, and die. Chestnut blight fungus and Dutch elm disease are examples of blights that affect trees.

ecological niche   The place or position within a plant's or animal's habitat to which it is particularly suited because of its specialized body parts, diet, and behaviors. For example, the ecological niche of a starfish is the oceans' rocky shorelines where it clings to rocks and eats shellfish.

fungicide   Any substance used to destroy fungi or the spores of fungi.

fungus   A member of a major group of simple living things that lack chlorophyll. Fungi include molds, rusts, mildews, smuts, and mushrooms. Some scientists also include bacteria in this group.

hyphae   The threadlike colorless filaments that make up the mycelium, or plant body, of a fungus.

mycelium   A mass of filaments (called *hyphae*) that form the food-gathering structure of fungi. The mycelium is embedded in a layer of soil or in a host organism.

ringworm   Any of several contagious diseases of the skin, hair, and nails of human beings and other animals. Caused by fungi, the diseases are characterized by ring-shaped discolored lesions covered with scales and blisters.

rusts   Parasitic fungi that produce spores the color of iron rust. Rusts occur on leaves, stems, and other plant parts from which they get their food.

smuts   Parasitic fungi that transform plants (especially cereal grasses) into dark masses of spores. The term also refers to the disease itself.

spores   Reproductive cells, or groups of cells, formed by certain plants, particularly ferns and fungi. Plant spores are produced in very large numbers, and under favorable conditions a new plant can develop from each spore.

ALTERNATE QUESTIONS

1. What would the effect be on human beings if all of the fungi on earth suddenly disappeared?

2. In spite of efforts to develop an effective fungicide, the chestnut forests of the United States have been destroyed by the chestnut blight fungus. Dutch elm disease, also caused by a fungus, has destroyed elms in North America and Europe. Ringworm and athlete's foot are common fungal infections in human beings. They are very contagious and difficult to prevent or cure. Rusts and smuts plague farmers. What characteristics of these fungi make them so difficult to control?

3. How are a fertilized chicken egg, a peanut, and a spore alike? How are they different? Describe as many similarities and differences as you can.

4. Centuries ago, people who observed large circles of mushroom growth in fields believed that they marked the paths of dancing fairies. They called them "fairy rings." How would a scientist today explain these rings of fungi?

CHALLENGE: Seeing Is Not Believing!

Science fiction movies and books sometimes feature imaginary plants and animals that have evolved only in the minds of the authors and directors. Most of these plants would be unrecognizable to a biologist. Sometimes they are given characteristics similar to human emotions: "Killer Vine Seeks Revenge on New York City." At other times the reproductive cycles of plants and animals are scrambled: "Spores from Alien Planet Hatch Space Creatures on Earth." Many authors ignore the fact that giant invertebrate animals such as ants or spiders would not be able to move in earth's gravity. Grown to the size of a house, their exoskeletons and flimsy legs would not be able to support their body weight. They would be unable to move or obtain food. In other cases, screenplay writers create massive green plants with giant leaves on barren dry planets.

1. Find and describe an example in a book or a movie where writers have taken considerable scientific license in creating a plant or animal. Explain why the organism is science fiction and not science fact.

2. Create and describe a frightening fungus, plant, or animal to star in a science fiction movie or novel. Base your creature on real (though possibly exaggerated) structures and life cycles. Title your movie and create a written advertisement and artwork to include in a newspaper.

5. I LAVA VOLCANO

INTRODUCTION

Features of the earth's surface are constantly changing, but these changes occur so slowly they are usually unnoticeable. Volcanoes are a dramatic exception that provide a natural laboratory for studying geological change. In this unit, students are introduced to the idea that the earth's present geological features are one stage in a continuing process of formation and erosion. They are asked to examine the relationship between these processes and the development of life forms on earth, as they hypothesize about the changes that would occur on earth without volcanic activity. Alternate questions focus on drawing conclusions about underground features based on observations at the earth's surface. The stereotype of a scientist in a white coat, peering through a microscope in a laboratory, is challenged as students are introduced to the exciting and often dangerous world of the volcanologist. A creative science challenge, with a social studies twist, is contained in a factual account of a tank of molasses that "erupted," flooding the streets of Boston, Massachusetts, in 1919.

QUESTION OF THE WEEK

Do volcanic eruptions serve any useful purpose? Over millions of years, what changes would eventually occur on the earth if all volcanic activity suddenly stopped?

Explanation

People are awed by the destructive violence of volcanoes, yet volcanic eruptions are of vital importance in the geological development of the planet. Most places on earth show evidence of volcanic activity in the past, although today over 60 percent of the earth's active volcanoes occur along the borders of the Pacific Ocean.

Volcanoes have been a major force in shaping the earth: forming mountains, islands, hot springs, geysers, and plateaus. Their ash has added nutrients such as phosphate and calcium to the soil, creating fertile farm land. Volcanic rock provides good drainage for rainwater and helps hasten the decay of organic material. Tungsten, gold, copper, and other valuable minerals have been transported from deep within the earth and deposited near the surface by volcanic eruptions. Productive mining operations are often located near volcanoes. Power plants use the heat produced by trapped magma to produce electricity. The constant upheavals of volcanoes help prevent the earth's surface from eroding into a flat plain that would eventually be submerged beneath the sea.

Points to Consider

Volcanoes have provided scientists with important information about how the earth was formed and about conditions in the earth's crust, mantle, and core. Some scientists believe that volcanoes have also played a key role in the development of life itself. The gases from volcanoes are the most probable sources of the oceans and atmosphere. The sea's salinity, the result of fumes from underwater volcanoes, must have been a vital factor in the evolution of life in the primeval sea. Without carbon dioxide, the principal gas emitted by volcanoes, photosynthesis could not have taken place. This means that there would have been no plants, no animals, and no human beings.

ALTERNATE QUESTIONS

1. **How are hot springs, fumaroles, gey-**

sers, and volcanoes related geological events? Show the relationship by drawing a labeled diagram.

Hot springs are areas of water in the upper parts of the earth's crust that have been heated by magma (molten rock) and hot gases from underground volcanic activity. When the thermal energy in the underground spring increases, hot water is forced into fissures in rocks. If the water reaches the earth's surface, it is forced out in jets of steam and boiling water through a narrow conduit. This narrow opening becomes blocked periodically by condensed minerals and other debris. When the pressure builds, water and steam often erupt explosively. This erupting water spout is called a geyser.

Fumaroles are cracks in the earth that vent water vapor and other gases continually. A fumarole occurs when the temperature in the underground water rises and the water is vaporized before it reaches the surface.

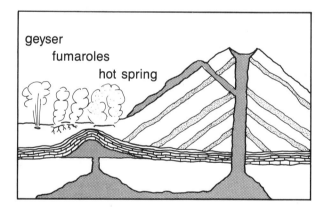

2. Geologic features such as mountains, lakes, rivers, and rock formations give scientists clues as to what might lie beneath the earth's surface. Imagine that you are on a scientific scavenger hunt. What geological features would you look for to find an underground source for geothermal energy, gold, and water? Where on earth could you find each item?

Geothermal energy is energy from natural heat trapped beneath the earth's surface. Magma is a source of this heat. Geysers and hot springs would be clues to sources of geothermal energy, since they occur where magma heats underground water. Iceland, Italy, New Zealand, and the United States are some of the countries in which geothermal energy plants are currently operating.

Minerals, such as gold, form deep within the earth's crust. Volcanoes often transport these minerals to the earth's surface where they can be mined. Therefore, it is likely that gold would be found in mountain chains formed by volcanoes. Gold found in the gold rushes in California and Alaska was a byproduct of the intense volcanic activity around the boundary of the Pacific Ring of Fire.

Underground water can be found almost anywhere on earth. In some places it bubbles just a few feet beneath the surface, frequently forming brooks, streams, and waterfalls that break the earth's surface. These brooks and streams are one clue to the presence of underground water. In other areas the water lies deeper within the earth's crust. Geysers and hot springs are evidence of subterranean water. Trees and other vegetation are also very good clues. In the desert, where little rain falls, lush trees often border dried streams. The roots of these trees have tapped a source of underground water.

3. Being able to predict volcanic eruptions and major earthquakes accurately would save millions of lives. In spite of years of research using sensitive equipment to measure tremors in the earth, geologists are still frustrated in their attempts to predict an earthquake or an eruption. Recently, some scientists have hypothesized that animals living near a fault in the earth's crust might provide some advance warning for human beings. Think of your own hypothesis to explain how animals might do this. Explain your reasoning. How could you test your hypothesis?

Answers will vary. In general, the hypothesis should be based on some way that animals might sense physical changes in the area near the fault. Perhaps they react to minute tremors that go unnoticed by human beings and seismographs. Perhaps there is a very high or low frequency sound before a tremor that some animals can hear. The hypothesis could be tested by observing measurable behaviors in one or more kinds of animals for some time prior to a quake. (The most active seismic area in the United States to conduct this research is central Nevada, a region that experiences about 5000 measurable earthquakes or tremors each year.) Students might hypothesize that the animals would appear more nervous, eat more or less, and/or move differently before an earthquake. Heart rates in mammals might increase or decrease. Differences before and after the quake could be analyzed to see if there was a noticeable change.

4. Scientists are often pictured in laboratories wearing white coats and conducting carefully designed experiments. Many people think the job of a scientist must be lonely and boring. In fact, most scientific research is exciting and sometimes even dangerous. Many scientists are part of a team. Some wear jeans and boots instead of white coats. For example, volcanologist David Johnson's research involved observing and recording the activities of Mount St. Helens in the state of Washington. His scientific observation post was about five miles north of the mountain's crater. On March 28, 1980, he predicted a coming volcanic eruption. He warned the public, "We're standing next to a dynamite keg and the fuse is lit. The problem is no one knows how long the fuse is." At 8:30 A.M. on May 18th, 1980, David Johnson learned the answer to that question. As Mount St. Helens erupted with an explosion 500 times more powerful than an atom bomb, he shouted into his transmitter "Vancouver, Vancouver, THIS IS IT!" Those were his last words. No trace of David, his jeep, or his trailer was ever found. Why would a scientist engage in such dangerous research? What scientists have jobs that would be exciting to you?

Some points that students may consider in forming an opinion are as follows: Many scientists engage in such research to gain a better understanding of the world and how it works. Often, the only way to gather needed data involves risks for scientists. Information gathered by these scientists often saves many lives. For example, if the data gathered on Mount St. Helens helps other scientists predict volcanic eruptions, millions of lives may be saved. Scientists take these risks because they believe the benefits that come from such research outweigh the personal sacrifices. Are these scientists heroes? Discuss the concept of heroism with students.

There are many kinds of research that might appeal to students as exciting. Some they might consider are aerospace research, cancer research, deep sea exploration, genetic engineering, psychological research into brain disorders such as split personalities, and environmental research on problems like acid rain and nuclear waste.

**CHALLENGE: A Case of
              Stick-to-itiveness!**

Answers will vary. Sample hypotheses might include:

- The type of metal used in manufacturing the tank was not strong enough to support the weight of the molasses. (The court ruled that this was the explanation for the disaster.)
- The extreme range in temperature was unexpected in January in Boston by the tank's designers. The seams ruptured due to failure to provide for expansion and contraction of the metal.
- The manufacturing process was at fault. Seams were not properly welded.
- The tank was structurally weakened previously when it was struck by a moving object of some sort.
- Continuous vibrations from passing trains had

weakened the seams and set the stage for a rupture caused by temperature changes.

- The tank was sabotaged by the owner who was losing money and wanted to collect on the insurance.
- The tank was sabotaged by a group of children as a prank.
- The tank was sabotaged by a rival molasses firm.
- The molasses fermented due to bacterial growth in the tank and then exploded from pressure caused by the fermentation.
- The tank was hit by lightning at some time in the past and structurally weakened.
- Woodpeckers had continually pecked at the tank, creating small depressions in the metal that eventually ruptured.

Firemen attempted to wash the molasses with water pumped by hand from water tanks on the firetrucks. This produced large sulfurous bubbles that filled the streets. Soap flakes were used to try to eliminate the bubbles. With freezing temperatures in January, the soap-covered molasses froze, increasing the problem. Some people tried to shovel and pick at the molasses with hand-made picks.

CHALLENGE TERMS

- **plate tectonics theory**   A theory that explains the apparent movement of the earth's continents. The theory suggests that the earth's crust is divided into about 20 separate plates that move independently above the earth's upper mantle. As these plates move, they carry the oceans and continents with them. The plates can collide with each other, move in opposite directions, or slip over and under each other. These movements cause earthquakes, volcanoes, and other geological phenomena.

- **pyroclastic debris**   Solid fragments such as chunks of rock and dust particles that are ejected forcefully from an erupting volcano.

- **shield volcano**   A volcano that forms as large amounts of lava flow quietly from fissures in the earth. These volcanoes have a broad flat base and a rounded dome-shaped peak. The Hawaiian Islands are an example of shield volcanoes.

- **stratovolcano**   A volcano with a cone-shaped peak and a funnel-shaped crater. Mount St. Helens is an example of a stratovolcano.

- **The Year without a Summer**   In 1816 the volcano Tambora, located on an island west of Java, erupted sending huge amounts of dust and ash into the atmosphere. For three days there was darkness for a distance of three miles. The layer of debris from the eruption was so thick that sunlight could not fully penetrate to the earth's surface. Temperatures around the globe were much lower than normal and snow was even recorded in some typically warm regions.

QUESTION OF THE WEEK

Do volcanic eruptions serve any useful purpose? Over millions of years, what changes would eventually occur on the earth if all volcanic activity suddenly stopped?

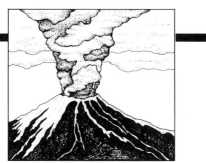

GLOSSARY

fissure   A deep, narrow crack in the earth's crust.

fumarole   A crack in the side of a volcano through which steam and gases rise. The steam and gases are caused by underground pools of magma.

geothermal energy   Energy from natural heat produced by the earth's hot core. Magma is a source of geothermal energy that produces steam to power generators in electric plants.

geyser   A special type of hot spring that erupts boiling water and steam at intervals. Contrary to popular belief, geysers do not erupt at precisely the same time each day.

hot springs   Boiling underground water that bubbles out of the earth creating surface pools. Hot springs are heated by underground reservoirs of magma.

magma   Molton rock that is formed by intense heat and pressure deep inside the earth. When magma reaches the surface of the earth and erupts from volcanoes or flows from fissures, it is called *lava*.

mantle   The area of the earth that lies beneath the crust and above the core, or innermost part, of the earth.

plates   Areas in the earth's crust that move separately over the mantle. Geologists believe that about 20 large plates support the earth's oceans and continents.

Ring of Fire   An area of intense volcanic activity that forms the boundary of the Pacific Ocean and all of the adjacent continents. The Hawaiian Islands are also part of the Ring of Fire.

volcanologist   A scientist that studies volcanoes—how they form, where they occur, and their basic chemical and physical structure.

ALTERNATE QUESTIONS

1. How are hot springs, fumaroles, geysers, and volcanoes related geological events? Show the relationship by drawing a labeled diagram.

2. Geologic features such as mountains, lakes, rivers, and rock formations give scientists clues as to what might lie beneath the earth's surface. Imagine that you are on a scientific scavenger hunt. What geological features would you look for to find an underground source for geothermal energy, gold, and water? Where on earth could you find each item?

3. Being able to predict volcanic eruptions and major earthquakes accurately would save millions of lives. In spite of years of research using sensitive equipment to measure tremors in the earth, geologists are still frustrated in their attempts to predict an earthquake or an eruption. Recently, some scientists have hypothesized that animals living near a fault in the earth's crust might provide some advance warning for human beings. Think of your own hypothesis to explain how animals might do this. Explain your reasoning. How could you test your hypothesis?

4. Scientists are often pictured in laboratories wearing white coats and conducting carefully designed experiments. Many people think the job of a scientist must be lonely and boring. In fact, most scientific research is exciting and sometimes even dangerous. Many scientists are part of a team. Some wear jeans and boots instead of white coats. For example, volcanologist David Johnson's research involved observing and recording the activities of Mount St. Helens in the state of Washington. His scientific observation post was about five miles north of the mountain's crater. On March 28, 1980, he predicted a coming volcanic eruption. He warned the public, "We're standing next to a dynamite keg and the fuse is lit. The problem is no one knows how long the fuse is." At 8:30 A.M. on May 18, 1980, David Johnson learned the answer to that question. As Mount St. Helens erupted with an explosion 500 times more powerful than an atom bomb, he shouted into his transmitter "Vancouver, Vancouver, THIS IS IT!" Those were his last words. No trace of David, his jeep, or his trailer was ever found. Why would a scientist engage in such dangerous research? What scientists have jobs that would be exciting to you?

CHALLENGE: A Case of Stick-to-itiveness!

On January 19, 1919, an eight-foot tidal wave of molasses swept down the streets of Boston, Massachusetts. Although there are no active volcanoes nearby, it must have appeared to residents of Boston's North End as though a volcano had erupted. The molasses "erupted" from a 50-foot holding tank, quickly flooding the streets and filling the basements with the black, sticky, sulfurous substance.

Read *The Molasses Flood* on pages 40 and 41, an account of the disaster. Formulate as many hypotheses as you can (at least 10) to explain why the molasses tank might have ruptured. Rank your hypotheses from most to least likely. Devise a cleanup operation to deal with the problem, using only the technology available in the year 1919.

The Molasses Flood: A Very Sticky Situation

by Alton Hall Blackington

As long as people work and live and play in the vicinity of North End Park in Boston, no winter will pass without someone recalling the catastrophe that took place there on January 15, 1919.

The scene of this tragic accident was that low-lying section of Commercial Street between Copps Hill and the playground of North End Park.

Looking down from Copps Hill on that mild, winter afternoon, you saw first the tracks of the Boston elevated—and the old, old houses nearby. Across the street were the freight sheds of the Boston and Worcester and Eastern Massachusetts Railways, the paving division of the Public Works Department, the headquarters of Fire Boat 31, and the wharves with patrol boats and minesweepers moored alongside. In the background to the left, the Charlestown Navy Yard. Towering above the freight sheds was the big tank of the United States Alcohol Company—bulging with more than two million gallons of crude molasses.

In the Public Works Department, a dozen or more horses munched their oats and hay, as flocks of pigeons fluttered around to catch the stray kernels of grain that fell from the feed bags. Stretched out on the running board of a heavily laden express truck, "Peter," a pet tiger cat, slept in the unseasonably warm sunshine.

This was the fourth day that the mercury of the thermometer on the sunny side of the freight shed had been climbing. On the 12th of January it was only two degrees above zero. But, on the 13th, the temperature rose rapidly from 16 degrees to 40; now, at 12:30 P.M. on Wednesday, the 15th, it was 43 above zero, and so warm in the sun that office workers stood around in their shirtsleeves (talking about the weather). Even the freight-handlers had doffed their overcoats, and sailors from the training ship *Nantucket* carried their heavy pea jackets on their arms.

Mrs. Clougherty put her blankets out to air and smiled at little Maria Di Stasio gathering firewood under the freight cars. She waved to her neighbor, Mrs. O'Brien, dusting her geraniums on a dingy window sill.

In the pumping station attached to the big molasses tank, Bill White turned the key in the lock and started uptown to meet his wife for lunch. He bumped into Eric Blair, driver for Wheeler's Express, and said, "Hello, Scotty. What are you doing around here at noontime? Thought you and the old nag always went to Charlestown for grub?"

The young Scotsman grinned. "It's a funny thing, Bill. This is the first time in three years I ever brought my lunch over here," and he climbed up on the bulkhead and leaned back against the warm side of the big molasses tank—for the first and last time.

Inside the Boston and Worcester freight terminal, Percy Smerage, the foreman, was checking a pile of express to be shipped to Framingham and Worcester. Four freight cars were already loaded. The fifth stood half empty on the spur track that ran past the molasses tank.

Mr. Smerage had just told his assistant to finish loading the last car when a low, deep rumble shook the freight yard. The earth heaved under their feet and they heard a sound of ripping and tearing—steel bolts snapping staccato, like a machine gun—followed by a booming roar as the

bottom of the giant molasses tank split wide open, and a geyser of yellowish-brown fluid spurted into the sky, followed by a tidal wave of molasses.

With a horrible, hissing, sucking sound, it splashed in a curving arc straight across the street, crushing everything and everybody in its path.

In less time than it takes to tell it, molasses had filled the five-foot loading pit, and was creeping over the threshold of the warehouse door. The four loaded freight cars were washed like chips down the track. The half-loaded car was caught on the foaming crest of the eight-foot wave and, with unbelievable force, hurled through the corrugated iron walls of the terminal.

The freight house shook and shivered as the molasses outside, now five feet deep, pushed against the building. Then the doors and windows caved in, and a rushing, roaring river of molasses rolled like molten lava into the freight shed, knocking over the booths where freight clerks were checking their lists.

Like madmen they fought the onrushing tide, trying to swim in the sticky stuff that sucked them down. Tons of freight—shoes, potatoes, barrels and boxes—tumbled and splashed on the frothy-foaming mass, now so heavy the floors gave way, letting tons of the stuff into the cellar. Down there the workers died like rats in a trap. Some tried to dash up the stairs but they slipped—and disappeared.

As the 58-foot-high tank split wide open, more molasses poured out under a pressure of two tons per square foot....

High above the scene of disaster, an elevated train crowded with passengers whizzed by the crumbling tank just as the molasses broke loose, tearing off the whole front of the Clougherty house and snapping off the steel supports of the "El" structure. The train had barely gone by when the trestle snapped and the tracks sagged almost to street level.

The roaring wall ... moved on. It struck the fire station, knocked it over on its side, and pushed it toward the ocean until it fetched up on some pilings. One of the firemen was hurled through a partition....

Up at fire headquarters, the first alarm came in at 12:40 P.M. As soon as Chief Peter McDonough learned the extent of the tragedy, he sounded a third alarm to get workers and rescue squads.

Ladders were placed over the wreckage and the firemen crawled out on them to pull the dead and dying from the molasses-drenched debris....

Over by the Public Works Building, more than a dozen horses lay floundering in the molasses....

Fifteen dead were found before the sun went down that night, and six other bodies were recovered later. As for the injured, they were taken by cars and wagons and ambulances to the Haymarket Relief and other hospitals....

Of course, there was great controversy as to the cause of the tank's collapse. About 125 lawsuits were filed against the United States Industrial Alcohol Company.

The trial (or rather the hearings) was the longest in the history of Massachusetts courts. Judge Hitchcock appointed Colonel Hugh W. Ogden to act as Auditor and hear the evidence. It was six years before he made his special report....

6. CURRENT EVENTS

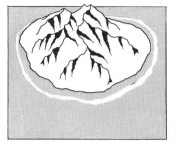

INTRODUCTION

Many naturally occurring events seem paradoxical; that is, at first glance they don't make scientific sense. These events provide students with an opportunity to learn that science is not random, that things happen for a reason, and that the reasons can be determined by observing, measuring, analyzing data, and drawing logical conclusions. Exploring the intriguing questions raised by such events often leads to a new and better understanding of basic scientific principles. In this unit, students will learn about wave motion and about the variables that affect wave patterns on beaches. They must put this information to use as they are challenged to design a future method of cleaning oil spills on the ocean.

QUESTION OF THE WEEK

If wind causes surface waves on the ocean, why do waves always flow towards shore on islands? Why are waves higher on one side of this island than the other?

Explanation

Ocean waves are caused primarily by wind from storms and air pressure variations at sea. Since waves travel outward from a storm center in all directions, it would seem that waves should come towards a beach from all angles. On some days we should even see waves that travel past beyond the shore and never strike the beach. We do not see such waves because a wave's speed decreases as it reaches shallow water. If a wave approaches a shoreline at an angle, the leading edge of the wave (the edge closest to the shore) reaches the shallow water around the island first. In shallow water the leading edge slows down. Since the rest of the wave in deeper water is still

traveling faster it catches up, causing the wave to break almost parallel to the beach. If you have the poster, this phenomenon is visible as the large waves breaking against Tahiti's coral reef curve in toward shore. (For a more technical explanation of this process, see Points to Consider.)

Another way to think about the question is to ask why there are waves on the leeward side (the side of the island sheltered from the wind) and why they are smaller. One explanation is that the smaller waves are generated by a different process. They are created by local breezes and gusts of wind. As these smaller waves reach shallow water around the sloping island, they also curve in towards shore for the reasons just described. These local water waves are present all around the island, although they are seen more readily on the leeward side of an island without the interference of the larger waves. Tidal surges also contribute to local water waves surrounding an island.

Points to Consider

Water waves are one example of energy waves. Sound, light, radio waves, radar, infrared, X-rays, and gamma rays are others. Light waves and water waves can be seen while most other waves are invisible. A water wave behaves like other waves. It can be reflected, that is, it can bounce off other objects it strikes directly. If it strikes an object like a sloping shoreline at an angle, it can be refracted—deflected from the path it was following. As a water wave reaches the shallow water around a beach, its wavelength becomes shorter. Since a wave's speed is a function of its wavelength times its frequency, any decrease in wavelength means a decrease in speed. If an entire wave is not moving at the same speed, it is refracted. Refraction occurs toward the part of the wave that is moving slowest. This is what happens when water waves reach shallow water.

The movement of water waves is often hard to understand because we can see the waves and they appear to move from place to place. In fact, the water particles themselves do not move from place to place. In the ocean, waves move through the water at a speed that is faster than the water particles. The water particles move in a circular motion as the wave passes by. Any object floating on the surface in deep water remains in the same position, regardless of the size of the waves.

ALTERNATE QUESTIONS

1. What is an undertow, or rip current? How does a rip current drag unsuspecting swimmers away from shore? What scientific information about shoreline waves would be helpful to a swimmer?

Rip currents, often called "undertows," occur when breakers cast large amounts of water onto shore in rapid succession. This water cannot drain easily back into the ocean. When the water reaches a certain height, a current starts and erodes channels leading away from the shore at varying angles. When these channels are large and drain with great force, they are called "undertows" or rip currents. The best advice for a swimmer caught in one of these currents is to remain calm and to avoid trying to swim directly back to shore against the flow of water. The current is usually of limited length and width. Eventually a swimmer will be able to swim parallel to shore and out of the current's grip.

Wave motion consists of a series of crests and troughs in succession. Water particles in the wave are carried forward on the crest and backwards in the troughs. Many swimmers mistake the natural backward movement of water in the trough for undertow. When waves break on steep shorelines or during high tide, this movement can be quite extreme. However, swimmers caught in the trough are soon carried forward on the crest and are not swept out to sea.

2. The word *tsunamis*, or tidal waves, strikes fear in people in certain parts of the world. What are they? What causes them? Compare tsunamis to regular ocean waves. Imagine that you are on an ocean liner in the middle of the Pacific Ocean and the captain reports that a tsunami is approaching the ship. Describe what you would expect to see as the wave gets closer.

The Japanese term tsunamis (tsoo-nom-ees) is commonly used by scientists to describe large ocean waves caused by earthquakes, volcanic eruptions, and landslides. In Japanese the term actually means "harbor waves." Tsunamis occur whenever there is an underwater vertical movement of large masses of rock. This vertical displacement causes massive amounts of water to be suddenly shifted up or down, beginning the rolling, powerful waves called tsunamis. In deep water, tsunamis are extremely long, low sea waves that move through the water at speeds of up to 600 miles (960 km) per hour. They often stretch 100 miles (160 km) from crest to crest but measure only a few feet from crest to trough and are almost invisible in deep water. Passengers on an ocean liner would probably not even notice this wave motion. When tsunamis reach land, however, wave heights can build to as high as 100 feet (30.5 m) before cresting and breaking. In contrast, a regular ocean wave is caused by winds at sea and not seismic events. It travels at speeds of up to 60 miles (96 km) per hour and is usually no more than 100 feet (30.5 m) from crest to crest. Although pounding waves erode shorelines and can cause floods and destruction inland, they are dwarfed by the destructive power of tsunamis. Over 36,000 people along the coasts of Java and Sumatra were killed by the tsunamis caused when the volcano Krakatoa erupted in 1883.

3. In spite of science, technology, and human determination to control the flow of water on the planet, the ocean still washes away houses and erodes beaches each year. Rivers feeding into the oceans flood their banks, destroying fertile farmlands and causing death and destruction. How have human beings attempted to control the

world's oceans and rivers? Identify and describe at least ten methods.

Building houses on raised concrete foundations above the high tide line is a common remedy in coastline communities. Methods used to control the ocean include dikes, sea walls, sand bags, breakwaters, and hurricane barriers that can be opened or closed to control the flow of water at high tide. The city of Venice in Italy even uses the ocean water to advantage by allowing it to flood the streets, providing waterways for transporting boats around the city. Dams, channels, reservoirs, and raised river embankments called levees are all mechanical solutions to the problem of inland river flooding. Land management techniques in the headwaters of rivers help control erosion and runoff that lead to floods downstream.

4. Science texts explain that water is not carried from place to place by waves. Instead, particles of water move in a circular motion as the wave energy passes through them. For example, a leaf floating on the water in the middle of the ocean is lifted up and then dropped back down in about the same place when a wave passes by. If this is the case, how can a surfer "ride" the waves into shore? How do floating bottles, driftwood, and seaweed ever get washed up on the beach?

In deep water the speed of a wave is greater than the speed of the water particles in the wave. That is why a leaf on the ocean remains in the same place as the wave motion first lifts and then drops it. However, as a breaking wave approaches shore, it slows. At this point the water particles have almost the same speed as the wave. A surfer rides the waves by moving at about the same speed as the wave. This is accomplished by staying with the crest of the wave where the water is moving fastest. A surfer also moves diagonally down the front of the wave as it breaks, using gravity to help maintain speed. If a surfer doesn't catch a wave as it crests, he or she will not be able to keep up with the speed of the wave and will be dropped like the leaf as the wave passes by. Most surfers solve this problem by lying on the board and paddling fast as a wave approaches. Seaweed, driftwood, and bottles are carried close to shore by ocean currents. Then they can be picked up on the crest of waves and carried into shore.

CHALLENGE: The Quicker Picker Upper

Answers will vary. Perhaps large solar-powered hovering aircraft will vacuum oil into holding tanks. Siphons might be used by sucking the oil down from the surface into underwater holding tanks. Some students may argue that oil spills will not be a problem one hundred years from now because the supply of fossil fuels will be exhausted. Challenge them to imagine a new environmental problem that people must solve and to propose a solution.

CHALLENGE TERMS

- **Bay of Fundy tide** The Bay of Fundy in Nova Scotia is famous because it has the world's largest tidal range. At the end of the bay, the change in water height due to the tides ranges from 46 to 51 feet (14–16 m) at various locations. High winds can add another 4–6 feet (1.2–1.8 m) to these figures. The range occurs because the natural oscillation of water in the bay is about once every 13 hours. This period matches the period of the tides. The combined motion increases the tidal surge.

- **propagate** To travel through space in a wavelike motion. The term is used to describe the movement of water waves like tsunamis, light waves, radio waves, and sound waves.

- **seiche** An oscillation of the water in an inland lake or sea. The water sloshes back and forth rhythmically creating small water waves. A seiche is caused by wind, landslides, underground currents, and seismic events like earthquakes. If an inland bay is almost completely closed off from the ocean, this movement can be set in motion by the incoming tide.

- **tidal bore** A surge of water that moves swiftly upstream headed by a wave or series of waves. Tidal bores form on rivers and estuaries near the coastline where there is a large tidal range and the incoming tide is confined to a narrow channel. When a tidal bore forms on a river, the direction of the river changes abruptly as the bore passes.

- **tsunamis** A series of extremely long and low sea waves generated by earthquakes, landslides, or volcanic eruptions. These events usually cause a vertical movement of large areas of rock in the ocean floor, heaving water up or down at the same time. It is this motion that sets a wave series on its way. They can travel at speeds of 600 miles (960 km) per hour and can reach heights of 50–100 feet (15–30 m) as they reach a shoreline.

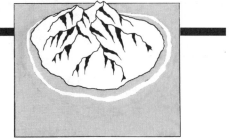

QUESTION OF THE WEEK

If wind causes surface waves on the ocean, why do waves always flow towards shore on islands? Why are waves higher on one side of this island than the other?

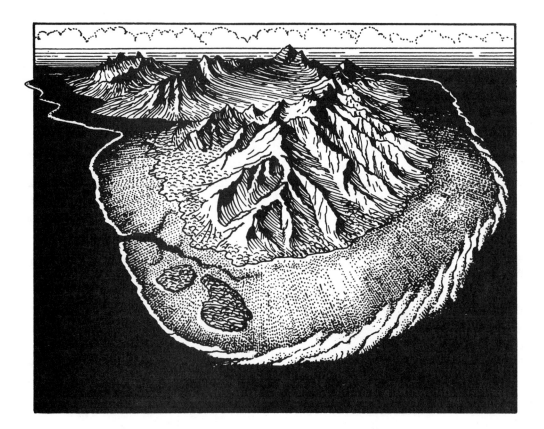

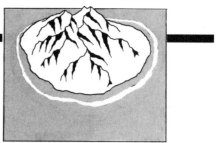

GLOSSARY

barrier reef   A coral reef roughly parallel to a shore and separated from it by a lagoon.

continental shelf   A shallow underwater plain that borders a continent and slopes steeply to the bottom of the ocean.

crest   The peak, or high point, of a wave.

leeward   Being in or facing the direction toward which the wind is blowing. Also, describing the side opposite of the windward side.

refraction   The change in direction or bending of energy waves. Water waves are one type of energy waves. Others include light waves, radio waves, and X-rays.

rip current   Commonly called an *undertow*. This is a strong surface current that results as waves break on shore and water rushes back to the ocean, often at an angle to the shoreline. Rip currents are strong enough to carry unwary swimmers out to deep water.

trough   The valley, or bottom part, of a wave.

wave   A rhythmic disturbance that travels through space or matter.

whitecap   White foam that appears on cresting waves. The foam is caused by brisk winds breaking the water's surface tension on the wave's crest.

windward   Being in or facing the direction from which the wind is blowing.

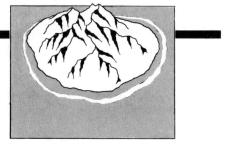

ALTERNATE QUESTIONS

1.   What is an undertow, or rip current? How does a rip current drag unsuspecting swimmers away from shore? What scientific information about shoreline waves would be helpful to a swimmer?

2.   The word *tsunamis*, or tidal waves, strikes fear in people in certain parts of the world. What are they? What causes them? Compare tsunamis to regular ocean waves. Imagine that you are on an ocean liner in the middle of the Pacific Ocean and the captain reports that a tsunami is approaching the ship. Describe what you would expect to see as the wave gets closer.

3.   In spite of science, technology, and human determination to control the flow of water on the planet, the ocean still washes away houses and erodes beaches each year. Rivers feeding into the oceans flood their banks, destroying fertile farmlands and causing death and destruction. How have human beings attempted to control the world's oceans and rivers? Identify and describe at least ten methods.

4.   Science texts explain that water is not carried from place to place by waves. Instead, particles of water move in a circular motion as the wave energy passes through them. For example, a leaf floating on the water in the middle of the ocean is lifted up and then dropped back down in about the same place when a wave passes by. If this is the case, how can a surfer "ride" the waves into shore? How do floating bottles, driftwood, and seaweed ever get washed up on the beach?

CHALLENGE: The Quicker Picker Upper

Ocean waves often carry oil spilled at sea towards land where it causes severe damage to coastline environments. Scientists have tried encircling and burning the oil, breaking its surface tension with soap, and soaking it up with huge quantities of chicken feathers. Scientists at a university in Texas have even developed a strain of bacteria that consumes oil. The bacteria can be stored in powdered form until needed and then sprinkled on the oil spill. After a few hours the oil disappears. However, in spite of all these creative solutions, oil spills are still a real danger to our shorelines and wildlife since each of the methods above has definite disadvantages for the environment.

How do you think oil spills will be handled 100 years from now? Design a technique or device for preventing future oil spills or for eliminating oil from the ocean once it has been spilled. Describe your method or device in detail and include a diagram or picture to show how it would work. Since the device must work in theory only, do not be limited by the materials or energy sources of the 20th century.

7. MOUNTAINS OR MOLEHILLS?

Earth Science

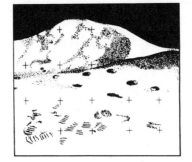

INTRODUCTION

Sometimes the absence of certain evidence can be just as informative to scientists as its presence. For example, many geological features on the earth are not present on the moon. Mountains on the earth show signs of present and past volcanic activity, while those on the moon do not. Scientists conclude from this information that the forces which shaped the earth's surface are absent on the moon. In this unit, students will explore the dynamic forces that result in mountain building on the earth. Using science in everyday life is emphasized as students are asked to identify all of the ways in which science knowledge would benefit a mountain climber. A geological puzzle provides science recreation for students as they attempt to identify and classify various high points and low points on earth.

QUESTION OF THE WEEK

If the earth and the moon formed at about the same time, why are mountains on the moon so smooth compared to the mountain peaks on earth?

Explanation

The forces that have shaped the geological features of the earth are not present on the moon. An atmosphere, the presence of liquid water, and active volcanism within the earth's crust and mantle are the most important forces that produce the jagged mountain peaks on earth. Wind and water erode its surface. Active volcanoes and colliding tectonic plates build mountains. There is a constant struggle between the active forces within the earth's crust and the destructive forces of its atmosphere. In contrast, the moon has no volcanoes and no atmosphere; it has been pummeled for ages by meteors that have destroyed its surface, leaving vast numbers of massive craters. The smooth mountains on the moon are actually the sides of these craters.

Points to Consider

The major mountain-building force on earth is the movement of plates in the earth's crust, a process that does not occur on the moon. The theory that explains the movements of these plates is called the theory of plate tectonics. Scientists have identified about 20 major plates, each thought to be about 62 miles (100 km) thick. These plates "float" on a layer of magma (molten rock), supporting the continents and oceans above them. Volcanic activity usually occurs where these plates collide, forming mountain ranges along their boundaries as massive amounts of rock are displaced. There is further evidence on the ocean floor to support this theory. The plates that form the floor appear to be spreading apart, allowing lava to ooze from the cracks. This liquid then cools and hardens, forming part of the ocean floor. This kind of mountain building produces the underwater mountains (also called shield volcanoes) that form island chains such as the Hawaiian mountains. These mountains rise almost 6 miles (9.6 km) from the ocean floor.

ALTERNATE QUESTIONS

1. What determines the height of mountains? Why are mountains on Mars higher than those on Earth?

The intensity and duration of the forces that created each mountain and mountain range determine how high peaks rise. Mountain ranges that are formed by the collision of two plates in the earth's crust contain the highest peaks. The Himalayan range in Asia was formed this way. Mt. Everest, the highest land mountain in the world, is found in the Himalayas. Islands are mountain peaks whose base forms part of the ocean floor. Measured from base to peak, some of these mountains are higher than Mt. Everest. The force of gravity on the earth determines the upper limits of mountain heights. After a mountain's weight (mass) reaches a critical point, the pressure at the base of the mountain becomes so great that its rock foundation melts. Gravity on Mars is less than on Earth. This is one reason Olympus Mons on the planet Mars is so much higher than Mt. Everest. The forces of erosion on a planet also limit the height of mountains. On Mars where the atmosphere is thin, the effects of weathering on mountaintops are less than on Earth.

2. If warm air rises, why are the tops of mountains always cold? If cold air falls, why is Death Valley, California, a place with the snow-capped Rocky Mountains nearby, so hot?

The atmospheric pressure at the top of a relatively high mountain is much lower than at its base. As warm air rises into this region of decreased pressure on mountaintops, it expands and cools. Death Valley, 282 feet (86 m) below sea level, is the hottest place on the earth with a record temperature of 134°F (57°C). Temperatures can remain at 120°F (49°C), or more, for several days in a row. These extreme temperatures occur because the Rocky Mountains block cool humid breezes from the Pacific Ocean. The winds that eventually reach Death Valley have deposited all of their moisture on the western slopes of the mountains. The dry air becomes heated as it descends down the eastern slopes. This process creates the hot dry desert in the area of Death Valley. The surface temperature in the area is also increased by heat reflecting off the desert sand.

3. Why would a geologist look for ancient fossilized sea creatures and plants on mountaintops far from water? Identify two mountain ranges in the world where you might find such fossils.

Some mountains were formed when two plates in the earth's crust collided. If one of the plates was part of the base of an ocean, large sections of the ocean floor were lifted high above sea level. Sediment from the ocean floor and living plants and animals that inhabit such an area were also lifted above sea level as the mountain formed. Millions of years later fossils of this sea life can be found in these high mountains. Mountains in the Himalayas in Asia and the Pyrenees in Europe were formed by such a collision, and they show an abundance of fossilized sea life. They are so plentiful that in some places they can be picked up along mountain paths.

4. Why must a mountaineer be an expert in many areas of science? Identify at least 20 scientific facts or concepts that are useful in this sport and explain what role each one would play in a three-day climb.

Mountaineers must be experts in many areas of science in order to stay alive during their climbs. Some sample responses of scientific facts or concepts that would be useful are:

1. Atmospheric pressure decreases with increasing elevation. A supplemental supply of oxygen is required at certain levels.

2. Rocks vary in hardness and density. Foot- or handholds in soft sedimentary rock could pull loose, releasing a climber.

3. Temperature decreases as a function of altitude. Protective clothing will be needed at certain altitudes.

4. A pulley is a simple machine that can increase the amount of work that can be done over a given distance with a given force. A pulley is helpful in lifting food and gear up the side of sheer cliffs.

5. Dehydrated food contains the same nutrients as fresh food. Carrying dehydrated food decreases the weight a climber must carry.

6. A duck's feathers prevent heat loss by trapping body heat in air pockets within the feathers. Duck or goose down feathers can be used as insulation in sleeping bags and jackets by climbers.

7. Increasing the oxygen supply to a fire increases combustion. Cooking over a campfire can be regulated by blowing on the wood or coals to increase the flame.

8. A campfire requires oxygen in order to burn. One way to put out a campfire is to smother it.

9. At lower altitudes dew forms as moisture from the air condenses overnight. Equipment left out overnight is likely to be wet in the morning.

10. Water freezes at 32°F (0°C). Drinking water supplies will need to be melted if the temperature drops below this level for long.

CHALLENGE: Where on Earth?

Each of the following landmarks pinpoints the highest or lowest continental altitudes on six continents. Challenge the students to identify two more high and low points on the planet. For example, the lowest point in the Pacific Ocean is the Mariana Trench, 38,635 feet (11,776 m) below sea level, and the highest point in Antarctica is Vinson Massif, 16,864 feet (5144 m) high.

Asia
1. Mt. Everest, Nepal, Tibet—29,028 feet (8,848 m) high
2. Dead Sea, Israel-Jordan—1,312 feet (400 m) below sea level

South America
3. Mt. Aconcagua, Argentina—22,834 feet (6,960 m)
4. Valdes Peninsula, Argentina—131 feet (40 m) below sea level

North America
5. Mt. McKinley, Alaska—20,320 feet (6,194 m)
6. Death Valley, California—282 feet (86 m) below sea level

USSR
7. Mt. Elbrus—18,510 feet (5,642 m)
8. Caspian Sea—92 feet (28 m) below sea level

Australia
9. Mt. Kosciusko, New South Wales—7,310 feet (2,230 m)
10. Lake Eyre, South Australia—52 feet (16 m) below sea level

Africa
11. Kilimanjaro, Tanzania—19,340 feet (5,895 m)
12. Lake Assal, Dijibouti—512 feet (156 m) below sea level

Moon features: Answers will vary. Well-known lunar features include: Mare Tranquillitatis (Apollo landing site); Tycho, Copernicus, and Kepler (craters); Mt. Hadley (mountain photographed by Apollo 15 astronauts).

CHALLENGE TERMS

- **law of superposition**   A major principle in geology that states that strata, or layers of sedimentary rock, are arranged in order from the oldest rocks at the base to the youngest rocks in succeeding layers.

- **Olympus Mons**   A volcano on the planet of Mars. Olympus Mons, also called Nix Olympia, is the highest mountain in the solar system. It is about 15 miles (24 km) high, three times as high as Mt. Everest. Its base would cover the state of Missouri.

- **orogeny**   The process of mountain formation. The term is most often used in connection with mountains formed by the folding of the earth's crust.

- **Rouse belts**   Circular earthquake zones on the earth that were first noticed by George E. Rouse, a student at Colorado School of Mines, while studying a globe on which earthquake sites were marked.

- **subduction zone**   An area in the ocean where one plate in the earth's crust descends below another one. This zone is the site of many earthquakes.

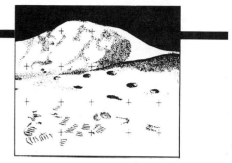

QUESTION OF THE WEEK

If the earth and the moon formed at about the same time, why are mountains on the moon so smooth compared to the mountain peaks on earth?

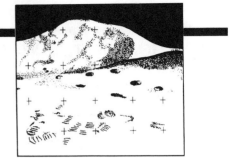

GLOSSARY

continental drift theory   The theory that the earth's crust is made of several different distinct sections, or plates, that move slowly over the earth's surface. Continents carried on these plates have drifted apart over the ages.

dome mountains   Mountains that form when magma (molten rock) is forced up under the earth's crust and hardens but does not break the surface. These mountains have rounded dome tops and a wide base.

fault-block mountains   Mountains that form when blocks of the earth's crust move up or down on one side of a fault.

folded mountains   Mountains that form when an ocean plate sinks beneath a plate carrying a continent. The land is forced up from such a collision and forms folded mountains.

fossil   Animal or plant remains or a trace of animals or plants found naturally preserved in the earth's crust.

mountain belts   Chains of mountains that run north to south along the borders of continental plates.

stratum   A sheetlike mass of sedimentary rock or earth of one kind (or age) lying between beds of other kinds.

tectonic plates   Plates in the earth's crust. These plates "float" on a layer of magma (molten rock) supporting the continents and oceans above them. Volcanic activity usually occurs where these plates collide.

topography   The study and description of the physical features of the earth's surface; also, the physical features themselves.

volcanism   The process of volcanic mountain building and eruption.

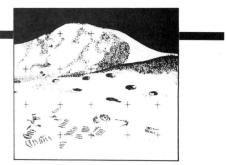

ALTERNATE QUESTIONS

1. What determines the height of mountains? Why are mountains on Mars higher than those on Earth?

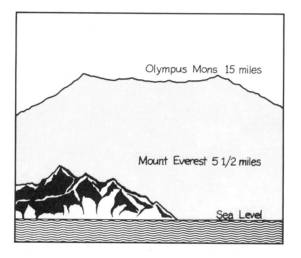

2. If warm air rises, why are the tops of mountains always cold? If cold air falls, why is Death Valley, California, a place with the snow-capped Rocky Mountains nearby, so hot?

3. Why would a geologist look for fossilized sea creatures and plants on mountaintops far from water? Identify two mountain ranges in the world where you might find such fossils.

4. Why must a mountaineer be an expert in many areas of science? Identify at least 20 scientific facts or concepts that are useful in this sport and explain what role each one would play in a three-day climb.

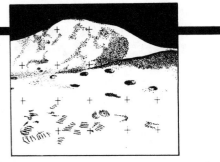

CHALLENGE: Where on Earth?

Each of the following regions should be familiar to a geologist. Identify each region and describe why the points marked with stars are famous "landmarks." (Map segments continue on the next page.) Which of the moon's features would you use as clues on a puzzle map of the moon? Identify five landmarks on the moon that aerospace geologists should recognize.

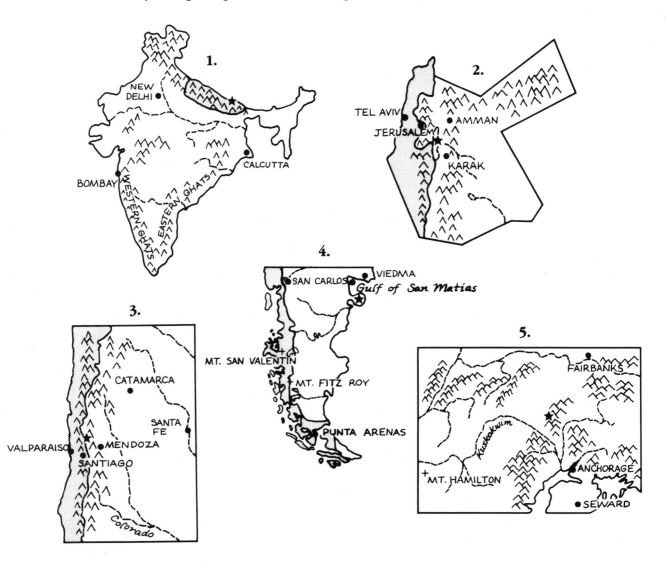

6.

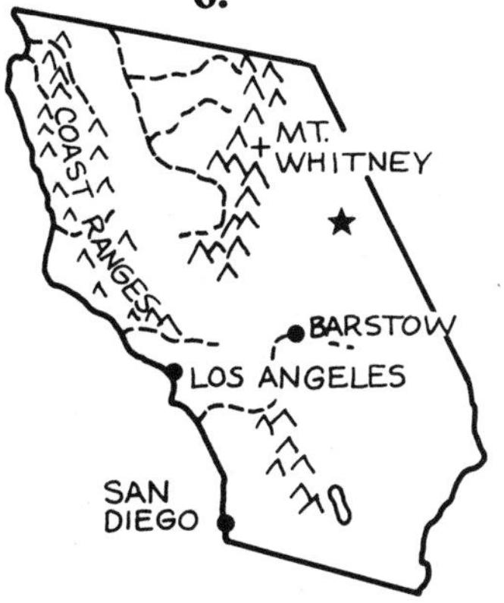
COAST RANGES
MT. WHITNEY
BARSTOW
LOS ANGELES
SAN DIEGO

7.

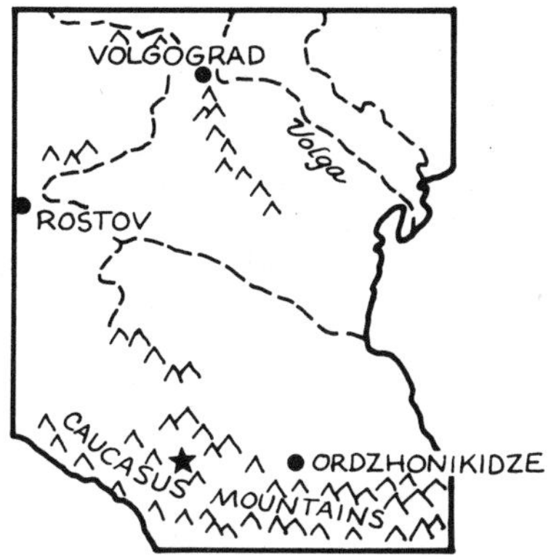
VOLGOGRAD
Volga
ROSTOV
CAUCASUS MOUNTAINS
ORDZHONIKIDZE

8.

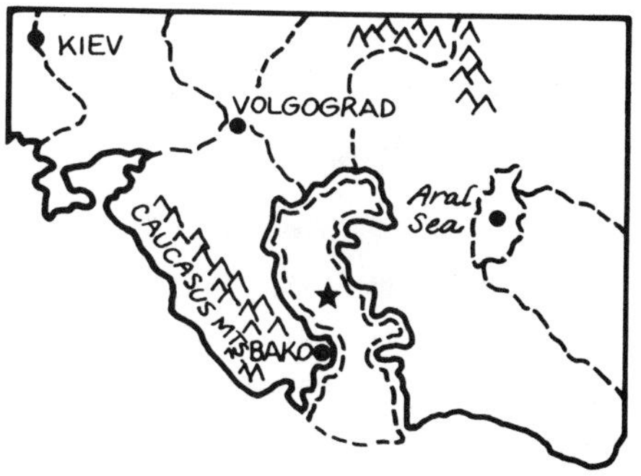
KIEV
VOLGOGRAD
Aral Sea
CAUCASUS MTS.
BAKU

9.

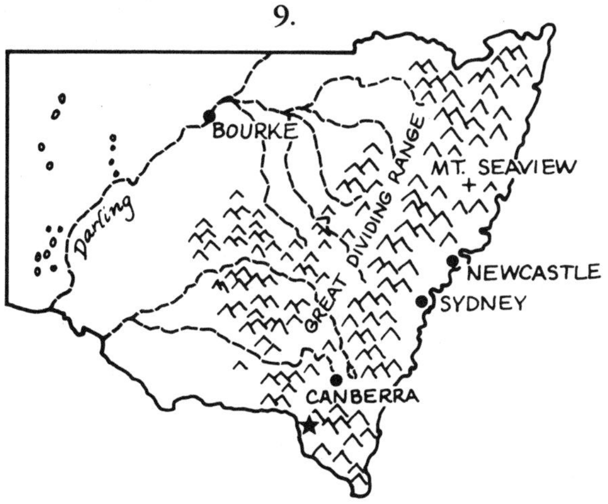
BOURKE
Darling
GREAT DIVIDING RANGE
MT. SEAVIEW
NEWCASTLE
SYDNEY
CANBERRA

10.

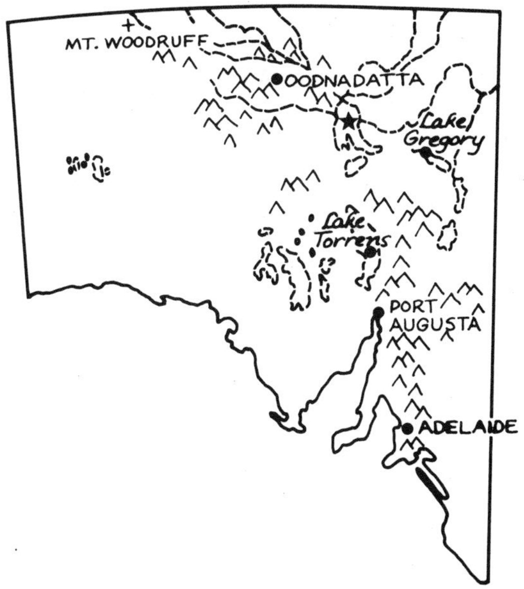
MT. WOODRUFF
OODNADATTA
Lake Gregory
Lake Torrens
PORT AUGUSTA
ADELAIDE

11.

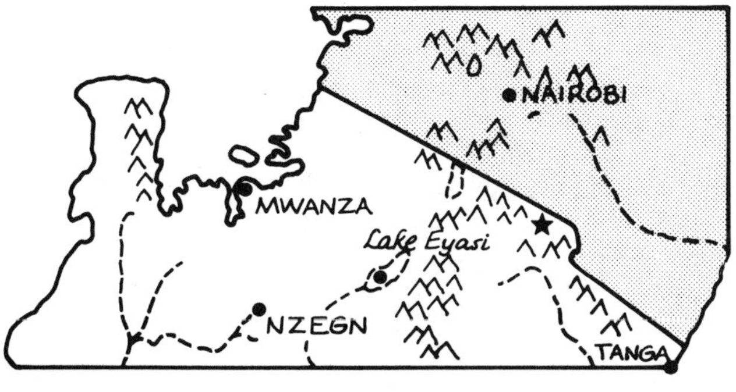
NAIROBI
MWANZA
Lake Eyasi
NZEGN
TANGA

12.

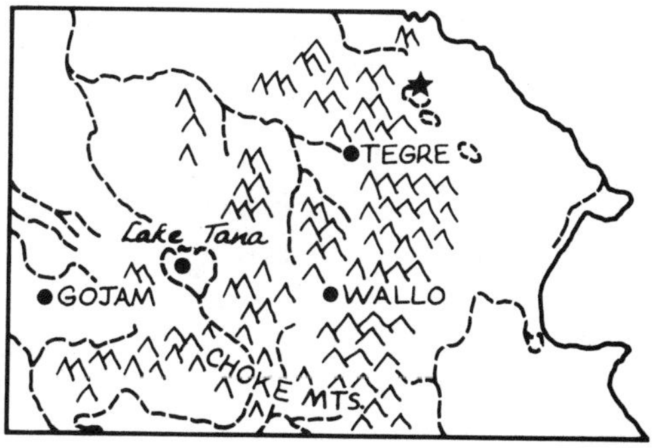
TEGRE
Lake Tana
GOJAM
WALLO
CHOKE MTS.

8.   COMET CULPRIT?

INTRODUCTION

How are scientific discoveries and technology related? How have scientists discovered so much about animals that became extinct 65 million years ago? Is there more than one hypothesis that explains the extinction of the dinosaurs? These questions are covered in the question of the week. In the alternate questions, students will explore the concept of geological time, and they will investigate various techniques that geologists and archeologists use to organize geological events into their proper historical sequence. The unit challenge requires students to synthesize all this information as they construct their own unique geological timepieces.

QUESTION OF THE WEEK

Why is it so difficult to determine what caused the extinction of the dinosaurs? What evidence supports the hypothesis that a comet caused this catastrophe?

Explanation

Since scientists must deduce what happened from fossil records, explaining any event that happened over 65 million years ago is difficult. Trying to explain the worldwide extinction of such vast numbers of animals in such a short period of geological time is especially hard. The fact that other animals alive at the same time as the dinosaurs survived must be explained. Many types of plants also survived. Sea life appears to have been less affected than life on the land. Any theory would have to identify the forces responsible for the devastation. Technology that allows geologists to date rock layers accurately and tests that provide highly accurate analyses of rock samples are now helping scientists identify those forces.

Nobel laureate physicist Luis Alvarez, geologist Walter Alvarez (his son), and physics professor Richard Mullen discovered large amounts of the element iridium in a 65-million-year-old layer of clay from Italy. They found the same large amounts of iridium when they checked rock layers of the same age at fifty other locations around the world. Since iridium is not normally present in such large amounts on the earth, they reasoned that the source must be extraterrestrial. A comet striking earth could explain the level of iridium. Dust and debris in the atmosphere from a large comet would have darkened the skies and lowered the earth's temperature enough to block photosynthesis in larger plants. Since plants are a critical link in the food chain, mass extinctions of animals would occur. One problem with this hypothesis is the fact that no crater of the right size or age has yet been found. Astronomers believe such a crater would have to be 60–90 miles (100–150 km) wide.

Points to Consider

Geologists have found that about every 28 million years the earth is bombarded by a large number of comets. Paleontologists report that over the last 250 million years fossil records show a high incidence of animal extinctions about every 26 million years. An intriguing new hypothesis proposed by astronomers suggests that our sun may have a companion star with a wide elliptical orbit. At its closest approach to the sun, the companion star's gravity would cause a large number of comets to leave the orbiting cloud and shower through our solar system. On the average, about 25 comets would hit the surface of the earth during this period, causing the mass extinctions recorded in the rock layers. The astronomers who proposed the hypothesis are now looking for a dwarf star about one-tenth the mass of the sun that would be about 2.5 light years away. If their hypothesis is correct, in 13 million years earth should experience a similar cosmic catastrophe.

ALTERNATE QUESTIONS

1. According to most scientists, what theory best explains where comets come from? If comets are just massive balls of ice and dust, why don't they melt when they encounter the heat from friction as they enter our atmosphere?

Most scientists believe there is a large "cloud" made up of millions of comets orbiting our sun far beyond Pluto. The cloud, called the Opick-Oort cloud after the scientists that proposed the theory, was formed from chemical elements in the earliest stages of the development of the solar system. According to the theory, the vast majority of these comets remain in eccentric orbits around our sun. However, if they collide with another comet in the cloud or are attracted by another star's gravity, they may slow in orbit. This may be one cause for comets drifting away from the cloud to be captured by our sun. Some of these comets are just propelled into outer space beyond the solar system and never return.

While most smaller meteors and other space debris entering the earth's atmosphere disintegrate, large comets would not melt completely. The heat from friction with the earth's atmosphere would melt only the outer layers of the comet. Millions of years ago some comets crashed into the earth's surface. Because of their size, on the average 6 miles (10 km) across, and the high speeds at which they travel, they left craters from 31 to 62 miles (50–100 km) across. One of the largest craters (87 miles [140 km] across) is located in Sudbury, Canada. We can see small fragments of comets burning up in the earth's atmosphere every time we watch a meteor shower.

2. Comets have been blamed for more than the extinction of the dinosaurs. How has each of the following persons, places, things, or events been associated with a comet? 1. Tunguska, Siberia, in 1908; 2. Sudbury, Canada; 3. Vredeforte, South Africa; 4. Noah; 5. Mark Twain; 6. Emperor Nero of Rome; 7. Bayeux Tapestry.

1. This area was devastated in 1908 by an explosion equal to the force of a hydrogen bomb. Scientists believe a comet exploded in the air over the site.

2. The suspected site of one of the largest impact craters on earth (87 miles [140 km] in diameter) caused by a comet.

3. The suspected site of another large crater impact, also 87 miles (140 km) in diameter.

4. Edmund Halley was one of many people who believed that a comet crashed into the ocean causing the flood that launched Noah's ark from its hilltop.

5. Mark Twain was born in 1835, a year when Halley's comet appeared. He died in 1910, the year it next returned.

6. Nero believed comets were signs of bad luck. When a comet appeared in A.D. 60, he had all of his successors put to death to ensure that his reign would continue.

7. During King Harold of England's reign, the Norman invaders conquered England. The King believed that the defeat was caused by the passage of a comet. This story was woven into the Bayeux Tapestry.

3. Sedimentary rocks are arranged in layers called *strata*. As sediment in rivers and streams builds up, rock layers form, one on top of the other. One of the basic principles of geology states that the lower strata of these rocks were formed earlier in time than the upper strata. Evidence from paleontologists supports this principle since fossils found at the same level are closely related. Also, fossil life in the lower levels is generally more primitive than that in the higher levels. Armed with this information and some library research, identify five errors in the diagram showing fossil distribution in a cross section of sedimentary rock.

Correct the errors by identifying the proper stratum for each misplaced fossil.

The misplaced dinosaurs and their correct placement are:
1. Stegosaurus—136 million years
2. Brachiosaurus—136 million years
3. Triceratops—65 million years
4. Pterodactylus—136 million years
5. Saltoposuchus—190 million years

4. Paleontologist James Jensen, nicknamed Dinosaur Jim, made a startling discovery in 1979. He found the 9 foot (2.7 m) scapula of a dinosaur in an ancient riverbed in Colorado. This dinosaur, which he named Ultrasaurus, is related to the Brachiosaurus. With only this bone, Dr. Jensen announced that he had unearthed the largest dinosaur ever discovered. Other paleontologists agreed with him. How can paleontologists tell the size of a dinosaur from just one bone? What other information can they learn by looking at a few bones?

Scientists deduce the dimensions of an animal by comparing similar bones of animals of the same species. In this case, Jim Jensen predicted the size of Ultrasaurus by comparing it with Supersaurus, which had shoulder blades of a similar shape. Knowing how large Supersaurus was allowed Dr. Jensen to predict the size of Ultrasaurus from the one bone he had. (Ultrasaurus stood 60 feet [18.3 m] high and weighed about 80 tons.) In addition to determining an animal's size and shape, paleontologists can determine how the animal moved by studying the shape and strength of the bones and joints of the skeleton, and they can determine what it ate by examining the shape of the skull, teeth, and forelimbs.

CHALLENGE: It's Time to Start Over!

Since the earth is about 4.5 billion years old, geologists and paleontologists do not measure time by the hour, day, year, or even by the century. Time is divided into eons: the Precambrian (the first 4 billion years of the earth's existence) and the Phanerozoic eons (the last 600 million years). Eons are subdivided into eras. Dinosaurs roamed the earth during the Mesozoic era, also called the Age of Reptiles. The Mesozoic era is subdivided into three periods. The Triassic period (245–205 million years ago), the Jurassic period (205–130 million years ago), and the Cretaceous period (140–65 million years ago). In the Triassic period the first mammal-like reptiles appeared on earth. During the Jurassic period the dinosaurs reigned supreme, and by the end of the Cretaceous period they became extinct. Although methods of telling geological time will vary, students should incorporate this information in designing their dinosaur timepieces. Sample designs may include a watch with a large hand that ticks off eras and a second hand that measures 10-million-year periods. Major fossils in each period may be arranged around the watch face. Don't limit creativity by suggesting responses to this question. Let imagination flourish.

CHALLENGE TERMS

- **Cenozoic era** One of three main eras that are important divisions in the history of life on earth. This era began about 65 million years ago and is still going on.
- **Cretaceous period** A division of the Mesozoic era that occurred about 130 million years ago. The dinosaurs died out at the end of this period.
- **Jurassic period** A division of the Mesozoic era beginning 180 million years ago. This period is also called "The Age of the Dinosaurs" because of the large number and variety of dinosaurs on earth at that time.
- **Mesozoic era** This era began 225 million years ago and ended 65 million years ago. This was the period of the dinosaurs and first mammals.
- **Triassic period** An important division of the Mesozoic era that started 225 million years ago and lasted for 45 million years. At the beginning of the Triassic period, the first dinosaurs and mammals appeared on earth.

QUESTION OF THE WEEK

COMET CULPRIT?

Why is it so difficult to determine what caused the extinction of the dinosaurs? What evidence supports the hypothesis that a comet caused this catastrophe?

GLOSSARY

aeon   (also eon) A unit of time equal to one billion years.

era   A major division of geological time. There are 6 eras; Azoic, Archeozoic, Proterozoic, Paleozoic, Mesozoic, and Cenozoic. Eras are divided into periods, and periods are divided into epochs.

extinction   The process in which entire species of plants or animals cease to exist on earth.

extraterrestrial   Originating or existing beyond the earth's atmosphere. Meteors and comets are extraterrestrial objects.

fossil   Animal or plant remains or a trace of animals or plants found naturally preserved in the earth's crust.

iridium   A silver-white, hard, brittle, metallic element that is very heavy.

paleontologist   A scientist who studies the life of past geological periods from fossil remains.

scapula   The shoulder blade, which is a major bone in the back. This bone is attached to many muscles that are used to move the arm.

sedimentary rock   Rocks that are produced by the accumulation of rock waste (called *sediment*) at the earth's surface.

strata   Sheetlike masses of sedimentary rock of one kind lying between beds of other kinds.

ALTERNATE QUESTIONS

1. According to most scientists, what theory best explains where comets come from? If comets are just massive balls of ice and dust, why don't they melt when they encounter the heat from friction as they enter our atmosphere?

2. Comets have been blamed for more than the extinction of the dinosaurs. How has each of the following persons, places, things, or events been associated with a comet? **1.** Tunguska, Siberia, in 1908; **2.** Sudbury, Canada; **3.** Vredeforte, South Africa; **4.** Noah; **5.** Mark Twain; **6.** Emperor Nero of Rome; **7.** Bayeux Tapestry.

3. Sedimentary rocks are arranged in layers called *strata*. As sediment in rivers and streams builds up, rock layers form, one on top of the other. One of the basic principles of geology states that the lower strata of these rocks were formed earlier in time than the upper strata. Evidence from paleontologists supports this principle since fossils found at the same level are closely related. Also, fossil life in the lower levels is generally more primitive than that in the higher levels. Armed with this information and some library research, identify five errors in the diagram on page 64 showing fossil distribution in a cross section of sedimentary rock. Correct the errors by identifying the proper stratum for each misplaced fossil.

4. Paleontologist James Jensen, nicknamed Dinosaur Jim, made a startling discovery in 1979. He found the 9 foot (2.7 m) scapula of a dinosaur in an ancient riverbed in Colorado. This dinosaur, which he named Ultrasaurus, is related to the Brachiosaurus. With only this bone, Dr. Jensen announced that he had unearthed the largest dinosaur ever discovered. Other paleontologists agreed with him. How can paleontologists tell the size of a dinosaur from just one bone? What other information can they learn by looking at a few bones?

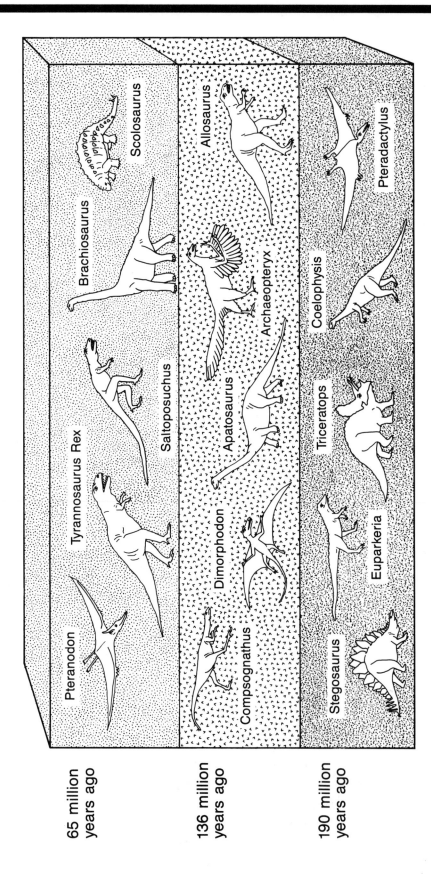

65 million
years ago

136 million
years ago

190 million
years ago

CHALLENGE: It's Time to Start Over!

In order to understand the world, scientists organize information in ways that are helpful in studying their particular field in science. For example, geologists and paleontologists have a special way of organizing the history of the earth. How do geologists tell time? Design a timepiece that would measure the passage of geological time during the period the dinosaurs roamed the earth. Since your timepiece must work in theory only, be as creative as you can with your design. Use eye-catching art wherever possible on your timepiece. Provide a description of how it keeps time and what the units of time mean.

9. SCIENCE FRICTION

INTRODUCTION

Technological advances depend upon an understanding of fundamental scientific concepts. Students explore the relationship between science and technology as they analyze a race car's design and performance in terms of aerodynamics and the physical forces of lift, thrust, drag, and friction. In the alternate questions, students must apply these same concepts to bicycle design and to common driving problems such as hydroplaning. Designing a new vehicle to use on the moon or Mars requires students to think creatively about the requirements of travel on extraterrestrial surfaces. As they incorporate features that best meet the needs of the new environment, they are required to suspend common conceptions of earthly machines.

QUESTION OF THE WEEK

What forces affect a race car's speed on the track? How are modern race cars designed and driven to maximize speed?

Explanation

The basic force that moves a car around a race track is the thrust from the car's engine. The amount of thrust is a function of the horsepower provided by the engine. The speed at which a car travels around a race track is determined by aerodynamic forces such as lift, thrust, drag, and friction. The weight of the car and the type of fuel used can affect a car's performance. The heavier a car is, the more power it takes to move it around the track. As the car moves, it encounters drag caused by currents of air pushing against the car's body. Race cars that are low to the ground meet less air resistance and therefore produce less drag. These smooth, streamlined bodies re-duce drag by directing air currents over and around the car's body. The friction of the tires on the race track can reduce speed. Skidding and loss of traction result in lower speeds and possible loss of control. Wide, smooth racing tires are designed to reduce friction and to provide maximum traction. Other forces such as gravity, atmospheric pressure, and weather conditions such as temperature, wind, and precipitation also affect speed.

One way that race car drivers maximize speed is by "drafting" or following another car closely to take advantage of the vacuum created behind the lead car. This strategy increases speed by reducing drag on the second car. Another way is by using the banked curves on the track to increase momentum by riding high in a curve and then shooting down into the straightaway.

Points to Consider

Improvements in the aerodynamics of racing cars have resulted in cars capable of moving at speeds of more than 200 miles (320 km) per hour on an oval track. To produce such high speeds, efforts have been directed in two major areas in race car design: reducing drag by streamlining the car and increasing stability and maneuverability of the car at high speeds. Drag is also caused by the turbulence of the air as it fills the vacuum left behind the moving car. The less streamlined the car, the greater the space left to be filled and the greater the turbulence. The greater the turbulence, the less stable the car becomes at high speeds. Designers responded to the problem of streamlining by creating cars that are very low and flat. Race car drivers are no more than a few inches from the ground. While the low, wide, flat design was revolutionary in reducing drag, it had one major flaw that designers had to correct—the car's shape was very similar to an airplane's wing. The air rushing over and under the car's body created lift. The car's wheels made too little contact with the track and the driver would lose control. The wide aerofoil at the rear of the car counteracts the lift by creating a downward force when air is forced over it.

ALTERNATE QUESTIONS

1. Why are oval race tracks constructed so that the outer ring is at a higher level than the inner ring?

Without this type of curve, called a "banked" curve, centrifugal force would cause race cars to lose control at high speeds. Students can compare this force to the feeling they get on an amusement park ride that spins riders around in an open wheel. The faster the ride spins, the more riders are pushed to the outside of the wheel. On a banked track the race car is pressed into the roadway at an angle that maintains traction and control of the car. Although modern highways do not have the extreme vertical banks that race tracks do, they are also raised on turns and curves.

2. In aerodynamic terms, what advice would a designer of race cars give to a bicycle racer?

Answers will vary. Choose a cycle with a light, strong frame. Counteract wind resistance by making sure handle bars are as close to the frame of the bike as possible and are not jutting out into the wind. Buy narrow tires. Dress in tight-fitting, slick clothing for streamlining. When riding, keep the upper body down low, as close to the frame as possible. Keep the head tucked down to present as little surface as possible into the wind. Decrease friction and increase speed by keeping gears oiled. Use the force of gravity to advantage by leaning into a turn. Take advantage of the racing technique of drafting, which involves using the area of decreased pressure behind the forward bicycle to help pull the trailing cyclist along.

3. Drivers sometimes experience a problem referred to as *hydroplaning*. What is hydroplaning in an automobile? What causes it? How can drivers avoid hydroplaning?

A hydroplane is a small high-speed motorboat with a flat bottom that skims along over the surface of the water. The term has been adapted to refer to a car losing traction on a wet road and skimming over the surface of the pavement. The problem occurs when a thin layer of water on the road causes the tires to lose contact with the pavement. Excessive speed increases the possibility of hydroplaning. Some tire manufacturers claim that the pattern of tread on a tire can decrease hydroplaning by increasing contact between the tire and the road surface. Having tires checked periodically and decreasing speed in rain or icy weather will help eliminate hydroplaning.

4. Why are newer race cars designed to fall apart piece by piece in high-speed crashes? Wouldn't it be safer to have the car's metal body shield the driver in an accident? Describe eight more safety features in automobile racing, and identify the problems they solved.

Major sections of the car's exterior shell are designed to absorb the shock of a collision by collapsing separately and falling away from the car. As each piece collapses, it protects the driver from bearing the entire force of the collision and from being injured and trapped by the collapsing metal. Other major safety features include:

- six-point seat belts to hold driver securely in car
- aerofoil on the rear of the car that improves traction
- engine placed lower in car to improve cornering
- helmets to prevent head injuries in collisions
- fuel tanks made of bulletproof nylon
- cockpit fire extinguishers
- heat-sensitive receptors that release fire extinguisher automatically

- fire-retardant uniforms
- roll bars to prevent head injuries in open cockpits

CHALLENGE: One Giant Leap for Mankind

Advantages The Lunar Pogo Stick takes advantage of the moon's decreased gravity, the absence of an atmosphere, and the irregular lunar surface. Because it is propelled by compressed gas, the Pogo Stick conserves energy. The gas requires very little space, leaving more room for passengers and cargo. It has a much greater range than the Lunar Rover driven by Apollo astronauts.

Disadvantages NASA specialists who analyzed the design were uncertain of the effect accelerating and decelerating would have on the crew. While the inventors thought the ride would be "exhilarating," some scientists felt it might be nauseating for people. They also questioned the stability of the vehicle. Because of fast acceleration and high speeds, any malfunction and crash could cause serious damage to the cabins. In spite of these disadvantages, NASA is still considering a remote-controlled version of the Pogo Stick for use on the surface of Mars.

Lunar Racers Student designs will vary, but they should each incorporate features that utilize the decreased gravity and zero atmosphere of the moon. The vehicle should be able to negotiate the irregular lunar surface with minimum difficulty. Aerodynamic features would be useless on the moon. Safety features would change depending on the design of the vehicle. If a moon racer leaves the ground as it is propelled forward, student engineers would need to take precautions against accidental hard landings. Collisions with other vehicles would still be a problem to address in the racer's design. Refueling might be a problem depending on the source of energy for the racer.

CHALLENGE TERMS

- **centripetal force** The force necessary to keep an object moving in a direction toward the center of rotation.
- **hydroplaning** A condition of decreased traction with a wet road surface that causes skidding and loss of control.
- **torque** A turning or twisting force that produces rotation or torsion; an automobile engine delivers torque to the drive shaft.
- **velocity** A car's speed in a given direction over a given period of time.
- **vortex** Swirling circular currents of air (or water) rotating around a center of decreased pressure. Vortices (plural) of air are created by race cars as they speed around a track.

QUESTION OF THE WEEK

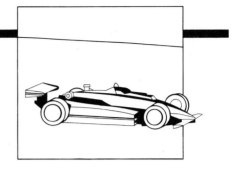

What forces affect a race car's speed on the track? How are modern race cars designed and driven to maximize speed?

GLOSSARY

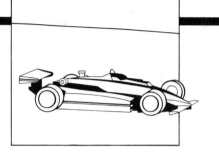

acceleration   The rate of increase in speed, or velocity, measured over time.

aerodynamics   The study of the motion of air and its effect on moving objects.

aerofoil   A wing or rudder of an airplane that directs the movement of air current and therefore controls the direction of the plane. In race cars, the wing on the rear of some cars that directs air currents down towards the ground, giving the car greater stability on the track.

centrifugal force   The force exerted outward from the center of rotation on a body moving in a curved path.

deceleration   The rate of decrease in velocity, or negative acceleration.

drag   The slowing force that acts in an opposite or parallel position on an object as it moves through water or air.

friction   The force that resists the moving of an object over the surface of another object.

streamlined   Designed to reduce resistance to motion through air or water.

thrust   The forward-directed force produced by airplane engines and rocket engines. The term is also used to refer to the acceleration of race car engines.

turbulence   Irregular motion of air currents.

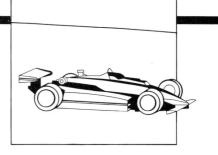

ALTERNATE QUESTIONS

1. Why are oval race tracks constructed so that the outer ring is at a higher level than the inner ring?

2. In aerodynamic terms, what advice would a designer of race cars give to a bicycle racer?

3. Drivers sometimes experience a problem referred to as *hydroplaning*. What is hydroplaning in an automobile? What causes it? How can drivers avoid hydroplaning?

4. Why are newer race cars designed to fall apart piece by piece in high-speed crashes? Wouldn't it be safer to have the car's metal body shield the driver in an accident? Describe eight more safety features in automobile racing, and identify the problems they solved.

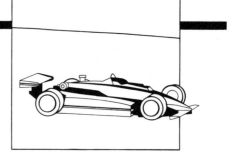

CHALLENGE: One Giant Leap
               for Mankind

Scientists expect that by the year 2010 people will be living and working on the moon. One problem facing these pilgrims from earth will be transportation. Scientists and inventors have already begun to design new and unique vehicles that take advantage of conditions on the moon. One of these is the Lunar Pogo Stick designed by Professor Howard S. Seifert with the help of Marshall Kaplan, an aerospace scientist. The basic design calls for two spherical cabins attached to a 60-foot (18.3-m) narrow cylinder of compressed gas. As the gas expands in the cylinder, the cabins are propelled upwards together reaching a speed of 100 miles (161 km) per hour in one second. The Pogo Stick makes a giant leap (200 feet or 60 m) off the surface and lands the length of three football fields away (300 yards or 91 m). At the end of the hop the cabins descend, compressing the gas in the cylinder. Once the gas is compressed, the Pogo Stick is pointed in the proper direction by the crew and is ready for another leap.

What problems would the Lunar Pogo Stick solve for moon residents? How does the Pogo Stick take advantage of conditions on the moon? What possible disadvantages might the vehicle have? Imagine that the sport of automobile racing is exported to the first moon base. How might moon racers differ from those on earth? Design a "lunarmobile" to enter in the Lunar Cross-Country. Describe the kind of power that would be used to propel the car and any special features that would make it especially suited for moon racing. Draw a picture or diagram of your entry. As you begin this challenge, remember the advice of Hermann Oberth, a German rocket expert who proclaimed, "The design of a moon car must not be influenced by tradition!"

INTRODUCTION

Even explanations of dramatic phenomena, such as lightning, can be broken down into bite-sized pieces by scientists. Through careful research, students will understand that the same basic concepts of static electricity that explain the shock from a doorknob can also explain the powerful jagged bolt of lightning in the sky. They must then apply these concepts in forming hypotheses about other situations involving static electricity. In the challenge activity, students can debate the merits of certain types of scientific research through questions such as "Why are scientists often labeled 'mad' by the public?" and "Why should the public support research if there is no practical application for it in the near future?"

QUESTION OF THE WEEK

Why are most lightning bolts jagged and uneven rather than straight? Why can we sometimes see lightning without hearing thunder?

Explanation

During a thunderstorm, the clouds and the earth become electrically charged. There is a positive charge on the earth, a negative charge on the bottom of the cloud, and a positive charge on the top of the cloud (see sketch). A typical lightning stroke begins with a pulse of current called a *pilot leader.* This is the first, nearly invisible flash that moves from the positively charged portion of the cloud to the negatively charged portion of the cloud. This flash creates a path that the rest of the stroke follows. Next, a stronger surge of current, called the *step leader*, moves along the path made by the pilot leader and then proceeds from the base of the cloud downward. The step leader, which is relatively faint and almost invisible, "jumps" toward the ground, pausing between each jump. Each time, negative charge from the cloud drains to the bottom of the path. There are pockets of positively charged air along the route. When the step leader runs into one of these pockets, it gets deflected. If a pocket is sufficiently strong, the leader may even be turned parallel to the ground! These deflections are what causes a lightning bolt to zig-zag across the sky. When the step leader is near the ground, a positive stroke shoots up towards it. The lightning bolt we see is the return flash moving back up the path left by the step leader.

We sometimes see lightning without hearing thunder because sound waves are easily deflected away from the ground (or refracted) by warmer air near the earth's surface. After a distance of about 15 miles (24 km), the sound wave is high enough from the ground that we are unable to hear it.

Points to Consider

While the leader stroke is moving towards the earth, the positive charge on the ground is building in strength. (Higher areas build up a higher charge. This accounts for the large number of lightning strikes on trees, telephone poles, church steeples, and people standing in the middle of open areas such as golf courses and baseball fields.) At a certain point, streamers of

electrical discharge rise up from the ground and connect with the leaders. Once the connection is made, a brilliant high-current flash, called a *return stroke*, moves back up the path. This flash illuminates the leader tracks, giving the impression that the lightning stroke is moving towards the earth. The whole process takes about one second.

ALTERNATE QUESTIONS

1. Why is an automobile a fairly safe place to be in an electrical storm? (Hint: It is definitely not because it has rubber tires!)

There is a common misconception that rubber tires insulate a car during an electrical storm. It is actually the car's metal body that provides the protection in a storm. Any electrical current striking a car is harmlessly conducted through the outer layer of the body. Passengers inside are unaffected by the current even if they are leaning against an interior car door. (However, it is best to avoid touching metal parts of the car since it is possible to be burned.) It is not safe to be traveling in a car when it could be hit by falling trees or electrical wires. An electrical wire sometimes falls on an automobile and continues to generate current electricity. Passengers are safe inside the vehicle. However, if they step out of the car while electricity is still flowing through the wire, they become conductors. They may be electrocuted as the current passes through them into the ground.

2. There is a common rule of thumb for estimating the distance between you and a lightning storm. Count the number of seconds that pass in the interval between the time you see a flash of lightning and the sound of thunder that follows. Divide the number of seconds by 5 to estimate the distance in miles. Divide by 3 to estimate the distance in kilometers. What scientific information was essential for the formulation of such a rule? How could you test the rule to determine whether or not it is accurate?

A flash of lightning is a powerful current of static electricity passing between objects of unequal charge. This current produces thunder by causing vibrations in air molecules. Light travels at 186,282 miles (299,792 km) per second. Sound waves travel much more slowly at about 0.21 mile (0.34 km) per second. Since the flash and the sound occur at almost the same instant, the difference between the time a person sees the flash and hears the sound occurs because of the distance the sound had to travel.

Any test that accurately measures the speed of sound would be a test of the rule. One test (devised in the 17th century) involved firing a gun at a distance from an observer. The observer recorded the exact instance of the powder flash from the gun and then recorded the exact moment when the report of the gun was heard. The speed of sound was determined by dividing the distance the sound traveled by the time elapsed. With modern equipment to produce sound and measure the distance it travels, more accurate measurements can be taken.

3. There are about 44,000 thunderstorms per day on earth. These storms produce over 8,000,000 flashes of lightning. Most of the flashes occur near the equator. Data from satellites indicate that ten times more thunderstorms occur over land than over the sea. Think of an hypothesis to explain this phenomenon.

Lightning is most often produced by towering cumulonimbus clouds. It occurs when there is a marked difference in electrical charge between the ground and the clouds or between two clouds. Cumulonimbus clouds form in warm, moisture-laden air fed by updrafts from the earth's surface. The formation of such clouds around the warm and humid equator is likely. Differences in air pressure create storms. These differences are likely to occur along coastlines. The storms then move inland.

4. Ranchers in the Rocky Mountains report that they receive painful shocks from touching wire fences during a blizzard. The shocks are sometimes strong enough to

knock men and cattle to the ground. Predict what might cause the shocks, and devise a way to test your prediction.

In general, students should base an hypothesis and a prediction on the principles of static electricity. Static electricity results when electrons from one object are transferred to another. A person walking across a rug builds up electrons that are transferred to a doorknob when a person reaches for it. The person feels a slight shock. The same process is at work on the fences. Metal fences bombarded by blowing and drifting snow particles become electrically charged. In a blizzard, large amounts of charge could build up due to prolonged blowing of the snow particles. The resultant charge would be many times more powerful than a simple walk across a rug. This would explain how ranchers and cattle could be knocked off their feet by the jolt.

Tests will vary and may include repeating the phenomenon in a laboratory setting, measuring the charge along the actual fence, and using a nonconducting fence.

CHALLENGE: Let There Be Light!

1. Robert Golka believes that ball lightning exists and can be harnessed as a cheap and limitless source of energy. He predicts that this is possible by creating ball lightning through thermonuclear fusion.
2. A pyrosphere is a device that uses five laser beams to create thermonuclear fusion. The reaction would supposedly be able to generate a million heat degrees in about 30 minutes. The pyrosphere would thus create "miniature suns," or ball lightning. Energy from these balls would be harnessed through collectors called "water jackets" and used to drive steam turbines. Deuterium, a hydrogen isotope available in large supplies in the ocean, would be used to fuel the reaction.
3. Answers will vary. To most people, research that is not based on traditionally accepted ideas is "mad." Scientific research that has little or no known practical application is also considered suspect by many people. Scientists who spend a lifetime devoted to such

activities are sometimes labeled "mad" because they do not conform to the social standards of others around them. They keep odd hours, appear uninterested in other topics, and are often labeled "absent-minded" because they pay little attention to details that seem important to others. Until recently, female researchers were often considered "mad" since science was "men's work" and any "normal" female would raise a family or choose another career.

4. Answers will vary. Encourage students to cite the advantages and disadvantages of such research. Some possible advantages: The research may produce a future source of energy. Even if it does not, it may answer some fundamental questions about the nature of ball lightning and will thus advance the frontiers of science. Disadvantages: The research is costly. The existence of ball lightning is still questioned. Efforts to harness a "theoretical" source of energy should be postponed in favor of known sources such as the sun, wind, geothermal energy, and synthetic fuels. Opponents of nuclear energy would question the need for a source of energy dependent on thermonuclear fusion.

CHALLENGE TERMS

- **bead lightning** Small luminous "beads" that appear along the channel of the lightning stroke. This form of lightning is very rare.
- **coulomb** A standard unit of measure of electrical charge equal to the quantity of electricity transferred by a current of 1 ampere in 1 second.
- **electrostatics** The branch of physics that deals with phenomena caused by the attraction or repulsion of electrical charges (but not movement of the charges as in current electricity).
- **fulgurite** A tubular piece of glassy rock created when lightning strikes sand or rock, melting and fusing the particles.
- **ribbon lightning** Ribbon-like streaks of lightning that occur when strong winds move the ionized path of the lightning stroke.

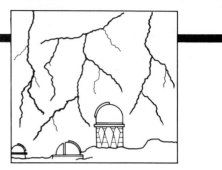

QUESTION OF THE WEEK

Why are most lightning bolts jagged and uneven rather than straight?
Why can we sometimes see lightning without hearing thunder?

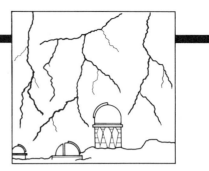

GLOSSARY

ball lightning   A luminous ball of about 20 cm in diameter that is reported to occur near the impact point of a lightning flash.

conductor   Matter through which an electrical current flows easily, such as copper.

cumulonimbus   A towering cumulus cloud formation that is often associated with thunderstorms.

current electricity   A moving electrical charge that occurs when electrons conduct a charge along a path of matter like a metal wire.

discharge   The equalizing of electrical charges (or potential) between two points or objects.

electrical charge   A measurement of the amount of electrons on an object; an excess of electrons is a negative charge, and a deficiency of electrons is a positive charge.

ground   To connect electrically to a large conducting body such as the earth.

luminous energy   Energy transferred in the form of visible radiation.

sonic boom   An explosive sound caused by shock waves, which form on the nose of aircraft traveling faster than the speed of sound (741 miles [1191 km] per hour), striking the ground.

static electricity   A stationary (static) electrical charge that builds up on an object due to the transfer of electrons from another object.

ALTERNATE QUESTIONS

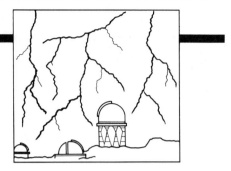

1. Why is an automobile a fairly safe place to be in an electrical storm? (Hint: It is definitely not because it has rubber tires!)

2. There is a common rule of thumb for estimating the distance between you and a lightning storm. Count the number of seconds that pass in the interval between the time you see a flash of lightning and the sound of thunder that follows. Divide the number of seconds by 5 to estimate the distance in miles. Divide by 3 to estimate distance in kilometers. What scientific information was essential for the formulation of such a rule? How could you test the rule to determine whether or not it is accurate?

3. There are about 44,000 thunderstorms per day on earth. These storms produce over 8,000,000 flashes of lightning. Most of the flashes occur near the equator. Data from satellites indicate that ten times more thunderstorms occur over land than over the sea. Think of an hypothesis to explain this phenomenon.

4. Ranchers in the Rocky Mountains report that they receive painful shocks from touching wire fences during a blizzard. The shocks are sometimes strong enough to knock men and cattle to the ground. Predict what might cause the shocks, and devise a way to test your prediction.

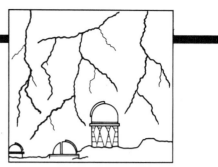

CHALLENGE: Let There Be Light!

Scientists and inventors often have a difficult time convincing people that their research is worthwhile. For example, the light bulb, the airplane, the telephone, and the rocket that launched the Apollo astronauts were all ridiculed by a disbelieving public. Read the following article about a scientist who is trying to harness the power of lightning. Then answer these questions.

1. According to the newspaper article on pages 80 and 81, what is Robert Golka's hypothesis?

2. What is a pyrosphere? How is it supposed to work?

3. In the opinion of one of the residents of Wendover, Utah, "Bob is either another Thomas Edison or a mad scientist." In fact, Thomas Edison was considered to be a mad scientist by many people. A physics professor, Henry Morton, in 1879 expressed the public's attitude about Edison and his light bulb when he asked, "How can Edison call it a wonderful success when everyone connected with the subject will call it a conspicuous failure?" Why are some people labeled "mad scientists" by the public? What triggers this reaction? Identify two other scientists or inventors who endured such ridicule. Describe their achievements.

4. In defending his research Robert Golka commented, "If you don't look under the rocks you will never find anything. I've looked under the rocks; I've found something. Now all I have to do is get the government or one of the big utilities to get interested in what I'm doing." Should the government or utilities support this type of research? Support your opinion with facts.

Lightning Tested As New Energy Source

by Charles Hillinger

Wendover, Utah—Robert Golka threw a couple of switches in the vast darkened hangar and—POW!—the building lit up like high noon on a sunny day.

Lightning bolts danced off the inside of the roof, sizzling, crackling and flashing eerily from a 20-foot-high coil.

"We're OK, so long as we stand our distance from the tower," Golka reassured his visitor. "But there is always that element of danger during my experiments. We've got to be careful not to get zapped."

Golka, 40, is one of the nation's leading lightning experimenters. He is credited with generating the most powerful lightning bolts ever created by man—flashes of 25 million volts that send off 50-foot sparks.

The scientist from Boston has been holed up for seven years, working in a huge abandoned World War II Army Air Corps hangar at the old Wendover Air Base in this remote village on the edge of the Great Salt Desert in western Utah.

The 750 residents of Wendover are not quite sure what to make of "the lightning man."

"Bob is either another Tom Edison or a mad scientist," one resident said, echoing the sentiments of nearly all those who live here. "Whatever, he's one helluva nice guy and smart as a whip."

Wendover says it's the only town in the United States with a lightning machine. Every child and nearly every adult in town has at one time or another stood in awe in the huge hangar, watching Golka do the lightning experiments.

Golka believes his man-made lightning is a key to a cheap and endless energy source.

"I have devoted all my energies the past 11 years to the study of lightning and to the goal of being able to reproduce ball lightning, one of the rarest and most mysterious phenomena known to man." Golka explained as lightning bolts bounced off the hangar's ceiling and floor.

Ball lightning is a stable hot gas phenomenon—a concentration of plasma resembling a soap bubble that occurs with lightning bolts on rare occasions.

"It can be a glowing sphere of a variety of colors, a half-inch or so in diameter or as big as a grapefruit," Golka said. "It is like an onion, with layers and layers of alternate charged particles, positive and negative.

"Sometimes the ball of lightning will bounce or float along through homes and buildings, lasting as long as a minute, then suddenly vanishing. It hums, crackles and hisses like drops of water on a hot stove.

"Sometimes it sets fires, sometimes it explodes. It has been known to kill people. Ball lightning knocked out the highly sophisticated electronic equipment in a lab at Hill Air Force Base (in northern Utah) three years ago."

Golka has asked the U.S. Energy Department to sponsor a major research program, directed by

him, to develop man-made ball lightning as a possible cheap source of energy.

"What I am proposing is a device I call the pyrosphere, employing five laser beams to create thermonuclear fusion," Golka said.

"The lasers would create an explosion in the air, producing a fusion reaction, getting up to 100 million degrees heat in a period of 30 minutes."

In essence, he explained, the laser beams would be creating miniature suns. The fuel would be deuterium, a hydrogen isotope.

"Energy would be collected through water jackets and used to drive steam turbines. The oceans (a source of deuterium) have enough energy to sustain the present use of power for the next 10 billion years turning turbines," Golka said.

He gave up a successful electronics business in Boston in 1968 when he moved to Utah's Bonneville Salt Flats.

The military long has been interested in his studies. For the last seven years the Air Force has allowed Golka to use the 60,000-square-foot hangar for $1 a year.

It is an historic hangar. It was built during World War II to house the B-29 Enola Gay, the plane that dropped the atomic bomb on Hiroshima.

Golka has had three grants totaling $68,000—one from the Navy and two from the Air Force—to test jet fighters for lightning vulnerability.

He zinged powerful lightning bolts at F-14 and F-16 fighters and other military aircraft to see if the planes were sturdy enough to resist lightning damage to their highly sophisticated computer systems.

The Air Force is talking to Golka about doing research on particle-beam weaponry.

"What I'm doing falls right into ray-gun research," Golka said. "I have already generated 25 million volts here in the hangar. I can get that up to 200 million volts with 200- to 300-foot-long sparks.

"By using laser beams I believe it will be possible to melt the skin of an ICBM missile, disarming and destroying it before it can reach its target. The ray gun would have a range of 6,000 miles.

"It would take a coil three times the size of the two combined coils I am working with in the hangar at the present," he said. One coil is 51 feet in diameter, the other is the 20-foot tower.

Golka said he would much rather help the energy program than devote his time and efforts to Buck Rogers-type ray guns, "but I can no longer do research solely on dreams."

"I am rapidly running out of funds. I scrounge dumps for materials with which to fabricate my equipment. I have already spent $100,000 of my own money on my research. . . ."

He has never married because "marriage and science don't mix when someone spends practically every moment awake on research."

He lives with his two mongrel dogs, Captain Proton and Commander Klystron, in a trailer. During the winter, when temperatures often drop nearly to zero in the unheated hangar, he bundles up in heavy clothing and keeps working.

"What I'm proposing is fusion, the combining of hydrogen atoms to form a helium atom. With fission—the splitting of heavy particles such as plutonium—there is always the very dangerous risk of radioactive byproducts. That risk is nonexistent in ball-lightning fusion," Golka insisted, adding:

"If you don't look under the rocks you will never find anything. I've looked under the rocks. I've found something. Now all I have to do is get the government or one of the big utilities to get interested in what I'm doing."

INTRODUCTION

Our ability to explain events depends upon the quality of the information we gather. Information-gathering skills become especially important in a situation such as the collapse of a bridge, where evidence may be destroyed or washed away. Scientists must then rely on "circumstantial evidence" to piece together the cause of the disaster. In the question of the week, students will become science detectives as they identify sources of information that might provide clues to the collapse of a bridge. In the process they will discover the importance of the data-gathering phase in scientific inquiry. Various bridge-building concepts and techniques are introduced in the alternate questions. Bridge building comes to the classroom when students are challenged to design a bridge of toothpicks and peas over a gap between two desks.

QUESTION OF THE WEEK

If you were director of the team to investigate why this Connecticut bridge collapsed, what information would you need to gather from witnesses, engineers, and state officials?

Explanation

Remind students that although they do not need to determine the probable cause of the collapse, they do need to gather all of the data that would contain the solution. You may wish to have them organize and present the information in an oral report, adding to a class list of information as each student presents his or her report. Point out that all scientists do not work in laboratories. Determining the reasons for the collapse of this bridge requires the expertise of applied scientists like engineers. Remind students that good applied and research scientists are among the best detectives in the world. They leave no stone unturned in their search for answers.

While students' answers will vary, a wide variety of sources and types of information should be included. Once they have completed their answers, challenge them to rank the information in order from most to least important and to predict what sources of information are most likely to contain the probable cause of the collapse.

(Information: Source)

1. condition of each part of collapsed bridge including debris from wreckage and pylons: engineers, metal specialists

2. last complete inspection report including the report itself, the name and qualifications of all inspectors, the date, the time of day, and the amount of time spent on the inspection: state officials

3. exact point of collapse: police reports, inspection by engineers

4. present condition of remaining bridge parts and embankments: inspection by engineers

5. exact date and time of collapse: police reports

6. engineering blueprints of the bridge including a report on all materials recommended for use in construction, and stress limits on all bridge parts: state officials, construction firm

7. average number of cars and trucks traveling over bridge daily: state reports, police

8. unusual sounds or problems noticed prior to collapse: nearby residents and eyewitnesses

9. weather at time of collapse: meteorologists, eye witnesses

10. list of materials purchased for use in construction: state officials, construction firm

11. condition of similar bridges: engineering and inspection reports on such bridges

12. estimated amount and condition of water flowing under bridge: tests by chemists

13. estimated amount of emissions from nearby factories: tests by chemists

Points to Consider

The driver of a tractor trailer and his passenger survived the collapse of the 25-year-old Mianus River Bridge, which occurred on June 28, 1983 on Interstate-95 near Greenwich, Connecticut, at 1:28 A.M. Three people in automobiles were killed. Engineers concluded that the probable source of the collapse was a broken pin in a metal hanger that held adjoining spans of the bridge together. Four of these pins, each one 10 inches (26 cm) long and 7 inches (18 cm) in diameter, bore the entire weight of one end of the span. The pin and hanger design allowed for contraction and expansion due to temperature changes. Before the bridge collapsed, residents reported hearing strange high-pitched noises coming from it that sounded like "thousands of chirping birds."

ALTERNATE QUESTIONS

1. Without doing any research, study the following diagram and explain how a caisson works. What engineering problem did the pneumatic caisson solve for bridge builders? (The diagram is on page 88.)

The pneumatic caisson originated in France and was first used by James Eads, who observed the technique on a visit there in 1868. Eads built the first railroad bridge across the Mississippi River in St. Louis, Missouri using a pneumatic caisson. This solved a basic bridge-building problem—how workers could anchor the supports of a bridge in bedrock in a deep and swiftly flowing river. The caisson provided air and a watertight chamber for working under water.

The pneumatic caisson is an open-ended rectangular or circular wooden box sheathed in iron or steel. It is constructed on land and then sunk into position under water. The very bottom of the caisson is open, and about 10 feet (3 m) up there is a watertight steel partition. This creates a chamber where people can work. Triangular pieces of iron form a cutting edge on the bottom of the box as the caisson sinks into a riverbed. The workers reach the air chamber through a hole in the caisson leading in from the top. From inside the chamber, workers dig into the riverbed and the material is carried to the surface through large pumps or dredging wells. As the riverbed material is excavated, more material is added to the shaft above, making it heavier. This helps the caisson sink. An air lock in the working chamber controls the air pressure. The flow of soil and water in the chamber can be modified by decreasing or increasing the air pressure in the chamber.

2. Many scientists believe that people will live and work on the moon in the near future. Will bridges be necessary on the moon? Describe how bridge building on the moon might differ from construction on the earth. What advantages and disadvantages might engineers have in bridging a large rift in the moon's surface?

Answers will vary. There will probably be a need for bridges on the moon because its surface is riddled with 3 trillion craters that are larger than 3.3 feet (1 m) across. Some are over 62 miles (100 km) in diameter. These can have 50-degree slopes on their rims. There are also many rilles (lunar trenches) that can be 124–186 miles (200–300 km) long and 0.25 mile (0.4 km) deep.

Advantages The decreased gravity on the moon would be an advantage in bridge construction. Girders and bridge spans could be made out of light, strong materials since they would not have to support the weight that bridges on earth do. Heavy machinery and equipment for lifting girders and other bridge structures would not be needed. Since there is no precipitation on the moon's surface and no oxygen, problems like rusting metal would be nonexistent in moon bridge building. There are no winds so aerodynamics would not be a consideration in bridge design.

Disadvantages Wide fluctuations in temperature might present problems since temperatures range from $-283°F$ to $+257°F$ ($-175°C$ to $+125°C$). Seismic recordings from the moon's surface show considerable disturbances when the moon is closest to the earth (its perigee) and farthest away (its apogee). This type of "tidal" activity is caused by the earth's pull on the moon. There are thousands of these moonquakes each year. Such seismic activity could eventually interfere with bridge supports. Selection of a proper site for bridge building and utilization of construction techniques that absorb the shocks would be important.

3. While bridges are not usually classified as works of art, to the engineers that design and build them they are masterpieces of science and technology. Choose a bridge that you would classify as a work of bridge-building art. Explain why your bridge is a masterpiece. Include artwork to show special features of the bridge. Describe the building concepts, techniques, technology, and materials that contributed to the construction of the bridge. Identify any problems engineers overcame in constructing the bridge.

Answers will vary. The roman arch, the pointed arch, steel, prestressed concrete, box girders, cantilevers, timber-trusses, bascules, the pneumatic caisson, cables, pontoons, and suspension spans are just a few of the design concepts and materials that students may identify.

4. While bridge collapse is rare in modern times, there have been some tragic examples of human error in bridge construction. In the state of Washington the Tacoma Narrows Bridge, nicknamed "Galloping Gertie," collapsed only four months after being opened to traffic. What caused the collapse and how could it have been prevented?

Opened to traffic on July 1, 1940, the Tacoma Narrows Bridge was the third largest suspension span bridge in the world. The bridge was 72

times as long as it was wide and had no stiffening support trusses. Instead it had a shallow solid plate girder along its edges. From the beginning the bridge had a strange flexibility that gave people the sensation of riding on a roller coaster. Workers building the bridge reported seasickness from the oscillations of the span. People came from miles around to enjoy the ride. Only four months after opening, however, the bridge's oscillations grew to catastrophic proportions. After several hours the bridge began to twist and gallop in both directions from a central point like a piece of ribbon candy. The bridge was cleared, and hundreds of people watched as it collapsed piece by piece. An understanding of aerodynamics would have prevented the collapse. The large vertical plates and the flexibility of the bridge were responsible for the oscillations. Air currents hitting the plates caused unequal pressure above and below the bridge spans. (See sketch.) These pressure differences caused oscillations that resulted in the bridge's collapse. If cuts had been made in the plate, the wind gusts and turbulence would have been reduced and the bridge would have been more stable.

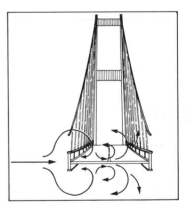

CHALLENGE: Bridging the Gap

This challenge can be used as an exciting engineering competition in class with teams of students challenging each other. Caution students that inserting too many toothpicks in one pea may cause it to split. It is better to start over when that happens. If any joints are weak when the structure is dry, a drop of white glue should correct the problem. The toothpicks and peas can also be used for these other challenges:

- Construct the tallest stable structure you can using 25 toothpicks and 50 peas.
- Construct the largest symmetrical geometric figure you can using no more than 30 toothpicks and 50 peas.
- Construct a model of an existing bridge using an unlimited number of toothpicks and peas.

CHALLENGE TERMS

- **bascule bridge**   A bridge, such as a drawbridge, that is counterbalanced by weights. Modern bascule bridges use small motors and a counterweight to raise or lower the bridge.
- **box-girder bridge**   A bridge constructed from hollow beams with a square or rectangular cross section. Box girders can be made of steel, prestressed reinforced concrete, or post-tensioned concrete. One example is the Rio-Niteroi Bridge in Rio de Janeiro, Brazil.
- **Caligula's bridge**   A bridge constructed in the first century A.D. by a mad Roman emperor, Caligula. Two rows of ships were placed side to side and connected with planks. The bridge stretched 3.5 miles (5.6 km) and served no purpose but to show off the emperor's unlimited power. He even had houses constructed on some of the ships so he could rest as he walked across the span. This ridiculous structure held the record as the longest bridge ever built for nearly nineteen centuries until 1927 when Lake Pontchartrain Bridge, in Louisiana, surpassed it at over 4.5 miles (7.2 km).
- **cantilever beams**   Beams that project out from piers towards each other and either meet in the middle forming a bridge or support a center span that connects the beams.
- **posttension concrete**   Concrete that has been strengthened by applying tension after the concrete has set.

QUESTION OF THE WEEK

If you were director of the team to investigate why this Connecticut bridge collapsed, what information would you need to gather from witnesses, engineers, and state officials?

GLOSSARY

bedrock   A layer of solid rock that is located beneath the soil. Bridges braced on land are anchored in bedrock for stability.

caisson   A pressurized watertight compartment used in underwater construction work.

civil engineer   An engineer whose training or occupation is in the designing and construction of public works, such as bridges or roads.

excavation   The process of digging out and removing material. Excavation creates a hole or cavity.

girder   A horizontal main structure on a bridge for supporting vertical loads.

oscillation   The state of swinging in a regular manner from side to side or back and forth.

pins   Pieces of wood or metal used to join together parts of a bridge. Also used as supports by which one piece may be suspended from another.

pylons   The towers that support the cables of suspension bridges. They typically form an archway at the approach to the bridge.

suspension bridge   A bridge that has its roadway suspended from two or more cables. The cables usually pass over towers and are securely anchored at both ends.

truss   An arrangement of wooden or steel beams that forms a rigid framework to support a bridge's roadway.

ALTERNATE QUESTIONS

1. Without doing any research, study the following diagram and explain how a caisson works. What engineering problem did the pneumatic caisson solve for bridge builders?

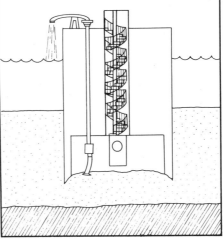

2. Many scientists believe that people will live and work on the moon in the near future. Will bridges be necessary on the moon? Describe how bridge building on the moon might differ from construction on the earth. What advantages and disadvantages might engineers have in bridging a large rift in the moon's surface?

3. While bridges are not usually classified as works of art, to the engineers that design and build them they are masterpieces of science and technology. Choose a bridge that you would classify as a work of bridge-building art. Explain why your bridge is a masterpiece. Include artwork to show special features of the bridge. Describe the building concepts, techniques, technology, and materials that contributed to the construction of the bridge. Identify any problems engineers overcame in constructing the bridge.

4. While bridge collapse is rare in modern times, there have been some tragic examples of human error in bridge construction. In the state of Washington the Tacoma Narrows Bridge, nicknamed "Galloping Gertie," collapsed only four months after being opened to traffic. What caused the collapse and how could it have been prevented?

CHALLENGE: Bridging the Gap

Use a box of 250 round wooden toothpicks and the following recipe for connectors to make bridge-building materials. With a maximum of 250 toothpicks and any number of connectors, build a bridge that will span a 2-foot (0.61-m) gap between two school desks of equal size. You may anchor the bridge to the desks using any non-permanent method. Test your bridge by seeing how much weight to the nearest ounce (gram) it can support across the opening. You can decide how the weight may be distributed, but at no point can the weights touch the desks.

BRIDGE CONNECTORS RECIPE

Ingredients:

1 bag of whole dried peas (available in the dried beans section of the supermarket—FRESH OR FROZEN PEAS CANNOT BE SUBSTITUTED)
water
1 tablespoon of table salt
plastic half-gallon ice cream container
1 box 250 round white or colored wooden toothpicks

Empty the dried whole peas into the plastic container. Cover the peas with approximately two inches of water. Mix in the salt. (The salt keeps most of the peas from sprouting if they are stored for a week or more.) Leave the peas uncovered for seven hours. If possible, stir once or twice as the peas absorb water and swell. Test the peas by inserting a toothpick halfway into the center of one pea. The pea should feel firm and should not break in half. Do not oversoak the peas. Drain any remaining unabsorbed water from the container. The peas may be used immediately or covered and kept in the refrigerator until needed or up to seven days.

Use the soaked peas to connect the toothpicks in the bridge structure of your choice. Leave the toothpick-and-pea constructions out to dry at room temperature on a piece of newspaper. As water evaporates from the peas they will tighten their hold on the toothpicks, producing a strong and rigid joint. Your structure may be spray painted when it dries. Gold or silver spray paint, or any iridescent color, is especially eye-catching.

12. A HOLE IN ONE

INTRODUCTION

Explanations of many phenomena are often counterintuitive, or contrary to what we would expect. For example, a parachute filled with holes works better than one without holes. In order to answer the questions in this unit, students must mentally experiment with ideas that don't seem feasible. Such experimentation by parachute inventors has led to step-by-step improvements in the stability of the chute. In researching the reasons for parachute design, students will learn basic principles of aerodynamics. Constructing and flying an object which, at first glance, resembles a paper tube challenges students to investigate the requirements for flight. Improving the tube's flight distance through experimentation provides an opportunity for students to systematically test and modify hypotheses about flight.

QUESTION OF THE WEEK

Isn't jumping from a plane risky enough without using a chute riddled with holes? Assuming parachutists don't have holes in their heads, what's the reason for holes in their chutes?

Explanation

The holes allow compressed air to escape and allow the chute to descend steadily. Without the vents, trapped air would rush from under the sides of the chute. This would cause the chute to swing drastically from side to side. A side panel that allows air to escape can also act as a method of jet propulsion. The stream of air coming from the panel pushes the chute in the opposite direction. These vents can be opened and closed with cords to steer the chute horizontally as it descends. This allows the jumper to land in a predetermined place and to avoid trees and other dangerous terrain.

Points to Consider

Students may soon see a new type of parachute on the market. The latest improvement in parachute design is a new spinning chute that will guide space vehicles to soft, accurate landings. Called a Rotating Flexible Drag Mill, the new design consists of twelve triangular pieces of material separated by gaps. The fabric strips slow an object's fall by producing lift. As air hits the triangular sections, the parachute spins counterclockwise. The spinning causes the chute to flatten out because of centrifugal force. This outward pull increases drag and makes the chute more stable. Another advantage of the new design is its size. The smallest model weighs less than half a pound (0.2 kg) and will fit in a pack the size of a 12 oz (0.36 L) frozen juice can. (See sketch.)

ALTERNATE QUESTIONS

1. Why shouldn't a parachute be opened at very low or very high altitudes?

Parachutes depend on air resistance for buoyancy as they descend through the atmosphere. At very high altitudes there is not enough air to support the chute. At very low altitudes the chute does not have time to fill with air and break the chutist's fall. A safe rate of descent is considered to be 20 feet (6.1 m) per second. The impact on the ground at that speed is like jumping from a height of eight feet. Sport parachutists have a limit of 2200 feet (671 m) as the lowest altitude for safely deploying the chute. At high altitudes, parachutists often free-fall for several thousand feet to reach denser air before opening the chute.

2. Many parachutes today are rectangular in shape. How does such a parachute work? Is this shape more or less buoyant than other shapes?

In general, a rectangular parachute works the same way that a conventional round chute works. The canopy provides enough air resistance to slow a parachutist's rate of descent. Some jumpers are convinced that the rectangular chute is safer and better because it is easier to control. There is enough air support to keep the chute as buoyant as other traditional shapes and less undersurface to catch gusts of winds that cause large oscillating movements and instability.

3. Some types of race cars use an open X-design parachute to slow the car after a high-speed run. Why don't they just use brakes?

Stopping a race car traveling at extremely high speed is not a simple task. Standard automobile brakes would burn up from the friction produced by pressure at high speeds. Maintaining control of the car at these speeds would also be difficult while braking. Unequal pressure on the

brakes would cause the car to skid or swerve. A parachute provides enough drag to slow the race car without causing it to skid. Just as the hole in a parachute prevents the chutist from swinging back and forth, the open X-design of the drag chute directs the flow of air very carefully behind the car to avoid any turbulence that would cause the car to swerve out of control.

4. Parachutes used to be constructed from one large piece of dull-colored fabric. Today's parachutes are designed so that separate strips (called gores) of brightly colored fabric are sewn together. Although these colorful chutes are beautiful as they fill the sky, the changes were made in the interest of safety. What problems do these safety features correct?

Any tear in a single piece of fabric would be disastrous for a parachutist. Air pressure pushing up on the chute could spread the tear throughout the chute. Depending on the size and position of the tear, the parachute could collapse as air rushed through a large, gaping hole. An accidental tear in one of the gores would be stopped at the seamline for the adjoining strip. This feature reduces the danger of the parachute collapsing.

The colors of the fabric are another safety feature. Although military chutes are camouflaged to protect jumping soldiers, most parachutes are brightly colored to make the chute easy to spot from the ground and easy for low-flying planes to avoid. If a parachutist is blown off course or lands in a tree, rescuers have little difficulty spotting the parachute.

CHALLENGE: UFO (Unidentified Flying Object)

Stationary air exerts pressure in all directions. When you throw the tube, thrust gives it its forward motion. As the paper tube moves through the air, it creates a faster flow of air over the cylinder. This creates an area of decreased pressure. The higher pressure under the tube pushes it up into the lower pressure region. These same forces of lift and thrust are responsible for the flight of airplanes.

Students interested in learning more about this

effect should investigate Bernoulli's principle, which states that the faster air flows, the lower the pressure it exerts.

CHALLENGE TERMS

- **anoxia** Lack of oxygen. At high altitudes parachutists can suffer from anoxia.
- **Bernouilli effect** Occurs when a liquid or gas flows around an obstacle or passes through a constriction. The effect is an increase in the speed of the flow and a decrease in the pressure against the wall.
- **momentum** A property of objects in motion. Momentum is the force with which the body moves against resistance. The amount of momentum depends on the mass and velocity of the object. For example, if a tennis ball and a baseball are traveling at the same speed, the momentum of the baseball is greater since it has more mass.
- **terminal speed** The maximum speed reached by a falling body. Once an object reaches its terminal speed it no longer accelerates but falls at a constant speed.
- **vortices** Swirling currents of air (or water) rotating around a center of decreased pressure.

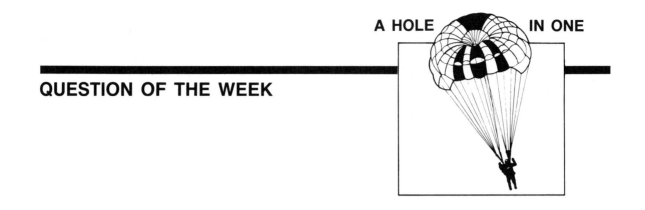

QUESTION OF THE WEEK

Isn't jumping from a plane risky enough without using a chute riddled with holes? Assuming parachutists don't have holes in their heads, what's the reason for holes in their chutes?

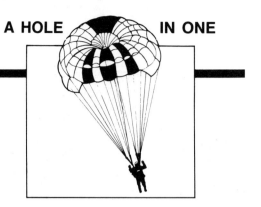

GLOSSARY

air resistance   The force of air against an object. A rocket is designed to reduce air resistance while a parachute's design takes advantage of air resistance. Drag on the body of a race car is another form of air resistance.

buoyancy   The upward forces on a floating object.

canopy   The fabric part of a parachute that catches the air.

free-fall   A fall through the atmosphere free from restraining forces; a parachutist's drop before the parachute opens.

gores   The separate strips of fabric that are sewed together to make up the canopy of a parachute.

harness   Leather or canvas straps that secure the parachute to the chutist's body. After landing a parachutist instantly releases the harness to prevent being dragged along the ground by wind filling the chute.

jet propulsion   The thrust produced when air rushes out from a panel in a parachute. The stream of air pushes the chute in the opposite direction.

oscillation   Swinging in a regular manner from side to side or back and forth.

stabilizers   Vents or openings in the parachute's canopy that regulate air currents and prevent dangerous oscillations. Without stabilizers, these movements are sometimes strong enough to tip the chute.

suspension lines   The lines that attach the parachute's canopy to the harness.

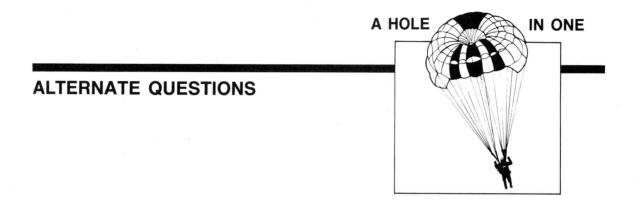
ALTERNATE QUESTIONS

1. Why shouldn't a parachute be opened at very low or very high altitudes?

2. Many parachutes today are rectangular in shape. How does such a parachute work? Is this shape more or less buoyant than other shapes?

3. Some types of race cars use an open X-design parachute to slow the car after a high-speed run. Why don't they just use brakes?

4. Parachutes used to be constructed from one large piece of dull-colored fabric. Today's parachutes are designed so that separate strips (called gores) of brightly colored fabric are sewn together. Although these colorful chutes are beautiful as they fill the sky, the changes were made in the interest of safety. What problems do these safety features correct?

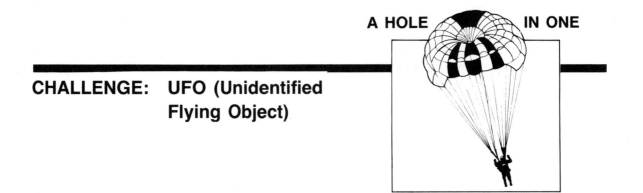

CHALLENGE: UFO (Unidentified Flying Object)

Follow the instructions below to construct a unique flying object with a hole running through it. You will need a piece of 8½ inch × 11 inch paper, cellophane tape, a pen or pencil, and a metric ruler.

When you have finished, fly the object by throwing it forward forcefully with a sidearm spinning motion. Why does the object fly? Try modifying the object to improve its flight performance. Name your UFO and challenge others in your class to a "Fly-Off."

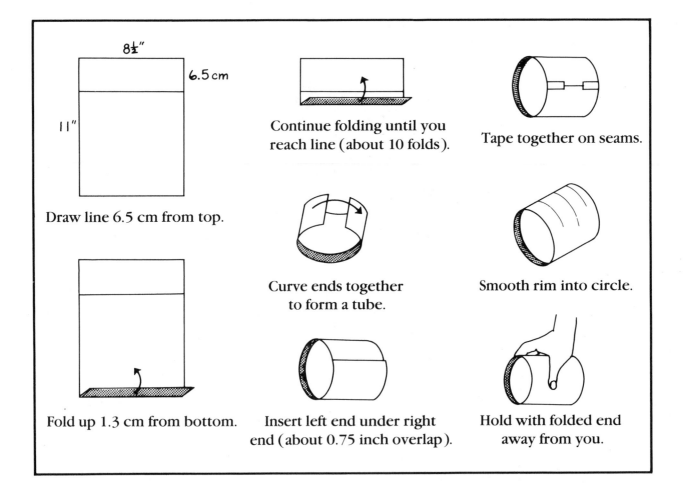

Draw line 6.5 cm from top.

Continue folding until you reach line (about 10 folds).

Tape together on seams.

Fold up 1.3 cm from bottom.

Curve ends together to form a tube.

Smooth rim into circle.

Insert left end under right end (about 0.75 inch overlap).

Hold with folded end away from you.

13. HOME AWAY FROM HOME   Aerospace Science

INTRODUCTION

How do scientists make decisions? What problems have scientists had to solve in order to travel comfortably in space? How has aerospace technology affected life on earth? In this unit, students are asked to find the answers to these and other pertinent questions about life in space. Choosing a limited number of plants and animals to accompany human beings to the first permanent colony in space provides students with an opportunity to weigh a number of variables before making a decision. In order to make a choice, the social, physical, economic, and biological requirements of each living thing need to be considered. In the alternate questions, students must identify the problems that modern products and technology have solved. Students are challenged to design a science experiment that takes advantage of the unique laboratory provided in the weightless environment of the Space Shuttle.

QUESTION OF THE WEEK

How will scientists choose the plants and animals to take on an interplanetary ark to the first permanent space colony? Which ones would rank in the top ten?

Explanation

While student answers will vary, it is important that they present some scientific evidence to support their choices. The colony would have to be relatively self-sufficient, with few imports and little or no wasted matter. Versatility would be a valuable characteristic for a colony plant. Students might consider its use as lumber, rubber, paper, and food for humans and livestock. Another function of plants is to provide oxygen and cycle moisture from the ground. Versatility is also important for the animals in the colony. Diet, size, reproductive cycles, habitat requirements, and domesticity would be some of the considerations in choosing animals. Symbiotic relationships between the living things imported to the colony are another important consideration. For example, flowers growing in the colony need insects for pollination. Bees need nectar from flowers to make honey. The aesthetic value of plants and animals should not be overlooked. Life without flowers, shade trees, bread, an occasional potato chip, chirping birds, and warm puppies would be hard to take!

Points to Consider

Discuss with students the advantages and disadvantages of including specific plants and animals. Corn, for instance, is one of the most widely grown crops on earth. It is used as food for livestock and as an ingredient in a variety of human foods. It can be made into syrup, oil, and alcohol. Corn plants can be grown using a technique called *hydroponics*, where plants are grown in water that has been enriched with nutrients. This would reduce the need for fertilizer and soil. Since the protein in corn lacks niacin, however, this important B vitamin would have to be supplied from another source.

Goats rank high on the animal list of some scientists. They can eat organic wastes because of the special microorganisms that they carry in their stomachs. It is estimated that the waste recycling unit on the space colony could be scaled down by half if goats were aboard. The goats would also provide milk, cheese, and meat.

ALTERNATE QUESTIONS

1. Aerospace researchers are experts in

scientific problem solving. The science and technology of sending people into space and making them comfortable and safe have produced many spin-off products for people on earth. How do each of these products and techniques solve problems that occur in space? Teflon, Velcro, aluminized Mylar, quartz oscillators, boilable bags, biotelemetry, and freeze drying.

- **Teflon** Teflon is a coating that was developed as a heat shield to protect spacecraft on re-entry. It is now used on common household items such as pots and pans.
- **Velcro** Velcro is a synthetic fastening material (with many tiny plastic hooks on one side and loops on the other) used to secure items in space cabins. This prevents things from floating around the ship.
- **aluminized Mylar** Aluminized Mylar is a highly reflective material, detectable by radar. It was developed as a covering for satellites so they could be easily located by radar signal. It is also used in spacesuits for its insulation qualities.
- **quartz oscillators** Quartz oscillators were developed for use on moon-flight missions that required pinpoint accuracy in liftoffs and landings. These oscillators are now also used in watches.
- **boilable bags** Boilable bags, or retort pouches, were developed as packages for astronauts' food. They provide a convenient way to store and cook meals.
- **biotelemetry** Biotelemetry is the technique of monitering bodily functions by radio transmission. It is used on spaceflights to check the health of astronauts. It is also used in hospitals and at-home patient care for the same purpose.
- **freeze drying** Freeze drying is a technique for drying food in a frozen state in a vacuum. The process solved the problems with storing food and preserving food on the spacecraft. A common example of the freeze-drying process is freeze-dried coffee.

2. **In a weightless environment, everyday** objects are often seen from unique angles, giving them an "out of this world" appearance. How in the world would you use each of these familiar objects?

1. screwdriver
2. binoculars
3. glue
4. toothpaste
5. notebook
6. earphones

3. **Many inventors and manufacturers are awaiting the day when objects used on earth have a "MADE IN SPACE" label. Products are already being designed for the time when colonies on the moon and Mars are home for earthlings. One such product is foamed metal. Foamed metal can be made easily in space factories by injecting millions of air bubbles into molten metal. On earth the bubbles would escape as the metal cooled, but in a weightless environment they are trapped inside. How could this light, super-strong metal be used on earth? Write an ad for a new or redesigned product that uses foamed metal.**

Answers will vary. The foamed metal could be substituted in the construction of almost any metal object. Manufacturers are planning to use foamed metal in buildings such as skyscrapers. Automakers will use the material in automobile frames where light but extremely strong frames would save energy and increase speed. Power-lines, streetlights, bicycles, and even eyeglass frames could be constructed from the metal.

4. **NASA scientists are now predicting that students who are in elementary and junior high schools in the 1980's will end up in jobs that do not exist today. Imagine that you are a citizen aboard a space station in geosynchronous orbit (see glossary) in the year 2025. What ten new jobs or professions will be needed that do not presently exist? What ten jobs that exist today are likely to have been eliminated by then?**

Answers will vary. Future jobs: bio-farming experts, space traffic control officers, solar array technicians, remote nursing technicians, video educators, bionics engineers, robotics salespersons, lunar miners, hydroponic gardeners. Outmoded jobs: mailroom personnel, machinists who are replaced by robots, bank clerks, small farmers, grocery cashiers, conductors on trains, doctors specializing in diseases such as cancer or heart disease, tobacco company workers.

CHALLENGE: An Uplifting Experience

NASA considers the following criteria to be important in selecting "Launch and Land" experiments to include on Shuttle flights. Share these with students before they begin this challenge activity. You may wish to use the point distribution recommended by NASA in providing feedback to students on their experiments.

Selection of Winners: All proposal entries will be judged by regional panels of NASA and other scientists, engineers, and educators. Up to twenty students will be selected as Regional Winners in each of ten geographic regions. As many as ten National Winners from the group of Regional Winners will be selected by National Judging Panels. All proposal entries will be evaluated on the following criteria:

1. Scientific Validity (10 points) The proposal concept, means of execution, and analysis are consistent with currently known and generally accepted principles in pure and applied sciences.

2. Suitability (10 points) The student has demonstrated the suitability of the proposal as a space science activity for the Space Shuttle Program.

3. Creativity and Originality (10 points) The student has developed a proposal that states a concept, a process, or an equipment design which demonstrates originality; or the student has de-

signed adaptations to equipment or a process used in previous space research for analysis to show originality.

4. Organization and Clarity (5 points) The student has described the proposed experiment according to the proposal elements.

Since the exact criteria for evaluating experiments may change, you may wish to contact NASA's Educational Services Office at any of the following locations for further information on Launch and Land, free classroom materials, and programs offered to educators.

- NASA Ames Research Center
  Moffet Field, CA 94035
- NASA Goddard Space Flight Center
  Greenbelt, MD 20771
- NASA Lyndon B. Johnson Space Center
  Houston, TX 77058
- NASA John F. Kennedy Space Center
  Kennedy Space Center, FL 32899
- NASA Langley Research Center
  Hampton, VA 23665
- NASA Lewis Research Center
  Cleveland, OH 44135
- NASA George C. Marshall Space Flight Center
  Marshall Space Flight Center, AL 35812

CHALLENGE TERMS

- **automaton** A mechanism that is relatively self-operating, such as a robot.
- **biotechnologies** Applied biological sciences, such as bioengineering, biofeedback, or anything that combines biology with technology.
- **electrostatics** A branch of physics that deals with static electricity, or electricity at rest.
- **scientific abstract** A summary of the main points of a scientific paper or report.
- **symbiosis** The close living together of two organisms of different species where the association benefits one or both of the organisms.

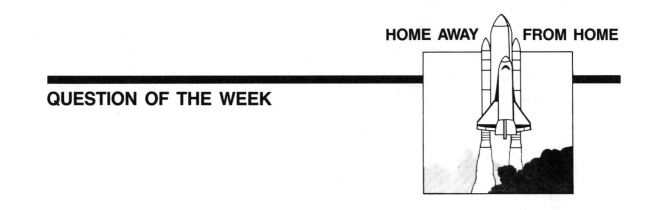

QUESTION OF THE WEEK

How will scientists choose the plants and animals to take on an interplanetary ark to the first permanent space colony? Which ones would rank in the top ten?

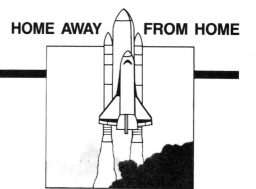

GLOSSARY

bionics   A science that tries to duplicate the sensing abilities of living organisms and to adapt them to human use through electronics.

biotelemetry   The remote detection and measurement of a condition, activity, or function of an animal, usually via a radio signal from a transmitter attached to the animal.

clone   Animal or plant produced from a single parent by any form of reproduction that does not involve the combination of male and female cells (asexual reproduction).

geosynchronous orbit   (Also known as **geostationary orbit**) An orbit above the equator at a speed such that one's position remains stationary over the same place on earth.

hydroponics   The growing of plants in a nutrient solution rather than in soil.

interplanetary   Between planets.

microorganism   An organism of microscopic size.

self-sufficient   Able to maintain oneself without outside aid; capable of providing for one's own needs.

ultrasound scanner   A device used for examining internal body structures. It emits waves at such high frequencies that they cannot be heard by humans.

versatility   The quality of having many uses or applications.

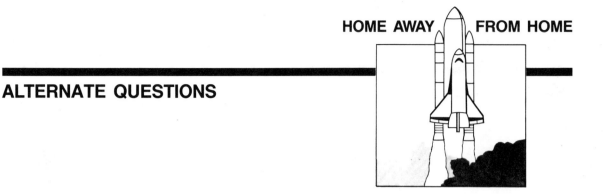

ALTERNATE QUESTIONS

1. Aerospace researchers are experts in scientific problem solving. The science and technology of sending people into space and making them comfortable and safe have produced many spin-off products for people on earth. How do each of these products and techniques solve problems that occur in space? Teflon, Velcro, aluminized Mylar, quartz oscillators, boilable bags, biotelemetry, and freeze drying.

2. In a weightless environment, everyday objects are often seen from unique angles, giving them an "out of this world" appearance. How in the world would you use each of these familiar objects?

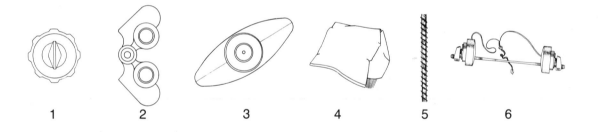

| 1 | 2 | 3 | 4 | 5 | 6 |

3. Many inventors and manufacturers are awaiting the day when objects used on earth have a "MADE IN SPACE" label. Products are already being designed for the time when colonies on the moon and Mars are home for earthlings. One such product is foamed metal. Foamed metal can be made easily in space factories by injecting millions of air bubbles into molten metal. On earth the bubbles would escape as the metal cooled, but in a weightless environment they are trapped inside. How could this light, super-strong metal be used on earth? Write an ad for a new or redesigned product that uses foamed metal.

4. NASA scientists are now predicting that students who are in elementary and junior high schools in the 1980's will end up in jobs that do not exist today. Imagine that you are a citizen aboard a space station in geosynchronous orbit (see glossary) in the year 2025. What ten new jobs or professions will be needed that do not presently exist? What ten jobs that exist today are likely to have been eliminated by then?

CHALLENGE: An Uplifting Experience

Scientists are anxious to use the weightless environment of space as a laboratory. Observing the behavior of matter in space can provide answers to questions about how and why things work the way they do here on earth. These experiments will also benefit people who will someday live and work in space. NASA has set aside room on Space Shuttle flights for experiments designed by students in high school. Each of the following experiments has been selected by NASA officials and science teachers to include on a Shuttle flight. Read each experimental abstract. What do you think each experimenter's hypothesis is? Design an experiment of your own for a zero-gravity environment. Save your experiment. You may want to submit it to NASA when you are a ninth grader.

1. "Cocoon-Spinning Behavior of Silkworms"
by Todd Egan (San Jose, California)

Earthbound experiments have already indicated that silkworms, in spinning their cocoons, employ gravity as an environmental clue. This experiment will observe the effects a zero-gravity environment will have on silkworms spinning cocoons in the Space Shuttle.

2. "The Effects of Heat, Light, and Zero Gravity on the Tunneling Habits of Earthworms"
by Scott Tyner (LaGrangeville, New York)

This experiment will compare the tunneling habits of 10 earthworms flown aboard the Shuttle with the behavior of 10 worms in a control experiment on earth.

3. "A Test of an Electrostatic Confinement in Space"
by William Akmentins (Huntsville, Alabama)

This experiment will determine whether an object can successfully be confined to a certain area using electricity in zero gravity, and if so, how much voltage it takes to keep the object in that area.

14. GLOBE TROTTERS Aerospace Science

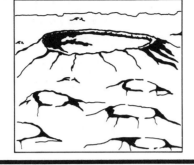

INTRODUCTION

The prospect of interplanetary travel has intrigued scientists for centuries. On the brink of the 21st century, as human beings are poised for travel to other planets, students should consider the scientific objectives of space exploration. As they compare conditions on Earth to those on the planet Mars, they are asked to identify some of the problems scientists will have to solve, and they will become familiar with technology and its role in advancing scientific frontiers. Creative problem solving and logical thinking are emphasized as students consider the consequences of drawing the wrong conclusions from scientific observations, as astronomer Percival Lowell did when he assumed that canals he observed on the Martian surface were created by extraterrestrial beings. To complete the unit, students are challenged to synthesize information in order to select a landing site for a future mission to Mars.

QUESTION OF THE WEEK

Why do many scientists support sending astronauts to Mars, even though the Viking probes found no signs of life on that planet?

Explanation

Answers will vary. According to astronomer Carl Sagan, scientists support sending astronauts to Mars because "A better understanding of Mars leads to a better understanding of our planet." For example, scientists are curious about the permafrost in Martian soil and the polar ice caps. They believe that chemical clues to the planet's past and to our own planet's history and development might be frozen in the soil and polar regions. They also believe that studying Martian weather (which is simpler than the Earth's) will lead to a better understanding of meteorological processes here. While the Viking probe uncovered no signs of life, many scientists feel that a human being would be able to locate better sites for study. Many support the Martian expedition because they think Mars may hold the answer to overpopulation on Earth. Some predict that Mars could be terraformed (planetary engineering to create an Earth-like atmosphere and environment) by melting the polar ice caps to create a warm, breathable atmosphere. Scientists have already demonstrated that primitive plant life could exist under present conditions on the planet.

Points to Consider

The Soviet Union is planning an unmanned mission to the Martian moon Phobos in 1988, with the possibility of a manned flight around the year 2000. Should it take place, the first United States mission to Mars would occur about 2010. The United States Mission, currently being considered by a group of supporting scientists and NASA officials, would involve the establishment of a permanent Martian base. The spaceship carrying the astronauts and their supplies would be so heavy (as much as 2 million pounds) that it could not be launched from Earth as one piece. Instead, it would be transported in pieces to a space station a few hundred miles above the Earth where it would be assembled and launched. The trip would take about seven months.

ALTERNATE QUESTIONS

1. Photographic evidence from the Viking probes shows that on a sunny day on Mars the sky is salmon pink. At night, the sky is

crystal clear and colored stars beam, rather than twinkle, in the heavens. Why is the Martian sky different from Earth's?

The Earth's sky is blue because sunlight is deflected by our atmosphere. The atmosphere acts somewhat like a prism. When a sunbeam passes through a prism, it is broken down into a rainbow of colors. The blue end of the rainbow is deflected most from the direction of the sunbeam. Air molecules in the atmosphere also deflect the blue light the most. Consequently, blue light rays come to the Earth from all parts of the sky and not directly from the sun. This is why on a clear sunny day the sky away from the sun looks blue. (In the vacuum of space, where there is no atmosphere, the sun's rays are not deflected. To an astronaut in space, the sky appears jet black.)

Mars has almost no atmosphere. During the day, heat currents from the sun cause high winds that swirl the iron rich red dust on Mars' surface into "clouds" that disperse the sunlight. The sky thus appears reddish pink. At night, when the heat currents disappear and the temperature of the planet falls, the dust settles. Without a dense atmosphere to distort the light waves, the stars shine steadily and appear different colors according to the temperature of the gases in the stars.

2.   **Terraforming on Mars is being considered by many scientists as a possible solution for the future food and space crisis caused by overpopulation on Earth. The Martian atmosphere is composed of 95 percent carbon dioxide, 2.7 percent nitrogen, 1.6 percent argon, and 1.5 percent oxygen. The temperature on Mars ranges from $-10°F$ to $+150°F$ ($-23°C$ to $+65°C$). Much of the planet is covered with permafrost. Gravity on Mars is about one-third as great as the Earth's. The day lasts approximately 24 hours. Hypothesize about the types of life on Earth that could survive in such conditions. Explain the reasons for your predictions.**

The atmosphere on Earth contains 78 percent nitrogen, 21 percent oxygen, 1 percent argon and other gases, and only 0.03 percent carbon dioxide. This means Earth's animals would not be able to survive in a thin atmosphere consisting of 95 percent carbon dioxide. However, plant life on Earth depends on carbon dioxide to make food through the process of photosynthesis, and nitrogen is also a nutrient that supports plant life. Therefore, some plant life could probably survive on the planet. To form a hypothesis about life under these conditions, students might consider the Arctic tundra with its harsh temperatures and permafrost. Experiments in which the atmosphere on Mars has been simulated on Earth show that primitive plants like algae and fungi can live and reproduce in these conditions. Some grasses survived the harsh environment but did not reproduce.

3.   **Imagine that after six months on the planet Mars, the first astronauts are preparing to return to the Earth. During their stay, they have observed no signs of life on Mars. Suddenly a black object the size of a large beach ball (3 feet or 0.91 m in diameter) with fluorescent green spots rolls over the horizon toward the landing module. As a scientist, what three questions, in order, would give you the most important scientific information about the object? Under what circumstances would you attempt to capture the object and return to Earth with it?**

This is a mental science puzzle for students. Answers will vary. Thinking each question through to its logical conclusion will allow students to acquire the most information about the object. A practical first question might be, "Is the object a threat to the mission?" If the answer is no, students' first scientific question might be, "Is the object alive?" Since the astronauts have seen no plant or animal life on the planet, this information might be obtained without wasting a question by using the logic: If the object were alive, it would obtain energy from some external source. On Earth, animals obtain energy by consuming other plants or animals in complex food chains. Since there are no other known living organisms on the planet, such a large object is probably not an animal, at least not one native to the planet. Therefore, a better question might be, "Is it a plant?" (The green spots could be part of a photosynthesis cycle in a plant.) Other possible questions: Can it respond evasively to obstacles in its course? What is propelling it? What is it made out of? Can it communicate with people? If it is alive and not a threat, consider the ethical problems that may arise from capturing it. For example, could it survive the trip to Earth, or would capturing it ensure its death? Do human beings have the right to interfere with life on another planet? (Perhaps the sphere is the last living member of a species.)

4.   The following headline appeared in *The New York Times* on August 27, 1911: "MARTIANS BUILD TWO IMMENSE CANALS IN TWO YEARS —Vast Engineering Works Accomplished in an Incredibly Short Time by Our Planetary Neighbors." How did the reporters and editors of one of the nation's most reliable newspapers make such an error?

Percival Lowell, a prominent American astronomer, observed the Martian landscape through a telescope and, along with other astronomers, reported seeing streaky markings that darkened during the Martian spring. He hypothesized that the streaks were canals that must have been constructed by intelligent beings. The Martian atmosphere, he reasoned, leaked water vapor into space leaving the air thin and the planet dry. The canals carried water from the polar ice caps (also visible through the telescope) to the equatorial regions of the planet where the Martian cities were. *The New York Times*, convinced that such a renowned scientist must know what he was talking about, published the article.

CHALLENGE: Mars or Bust!

Answers will vary. Factors influencing decision: relative smoothness of landing site, shelter from massive dust storms, probability of clear, steady communications with Earth, geological interest of the site, potential for setting up permanent base in the future. When the sites are selected, write a group letter to NASA asking for any information on preliminary sites for the manned landing.

Viking 1's landing site was in a region known as Chryse Planitia (at 22° north latitude, 45° west longitude on the map segment). There were a number of reasons for picking this site. It is an area of low elevation, which increased the chances of water being found; it is basically smooth so there was less danger in landing; it was in a position that allowed clear radar contact with Earth (a smooth surface is needed to reflect a strong signal). However, the composition and age of Chryse Planitia is less interesting than that of other areas. It was chosen as a "safe, but dull" landing site.

CHALLENGE TERMS

- **brecciate**   To form rock by the process of fragmentation and reforming.
- **eolian**   Borne, deposited, produced, or eroded by the wind.
- **fluvial**   Produced by stream action. The presence of fluvial deposits on Mars shows that there was once water in some form on Mars.
- **Giovanni Schiaparelli**   The Italian astronomer who first identified the dark lines on the planet Mars as *canali*, the Italian word for "channels." The mistranslation of this term as "canals" eventually resulted in the belief that canals were artificially constructed by Martians.
- **Chryse Planitia**   Viking 1's landing site on Mars.

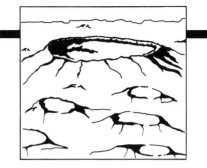

QUESTION OF THE WEEK

Why do many scientists support sending astronauts to Mars, even though the Viking probes found no signs of life on that planet?

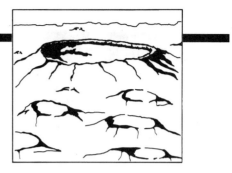

GLOSSARY

argon   A colorless, odorless gaseous element that occurs in the air and in other natural gas mixtures.

arid   Dry due to insufficient rainfall or moisture.

fluorescent   Bright and glowing as a result of electromagnetic radiation emissions.

habitable   Capable of supporting living things.

irrigate   To supply water to land by artificial means.

nitrogen   A gaseous element that makes up about 78 percent of the earth's atmosphere. It is odorless, colorless, and tasteless.

oxygenate   To treat, infuse, or combine with oxygen.

permafrost   A permanently frozen layer of soil that occurs whenever the air temperature remains below 32°F (0°C) for several years.

photosynthesis   The process by which plants make food. It occurs mainly in green leaves through the combination of carbon dioxide and water in the presence of light and chlorophyll.

terraforming   Creating an earthlike environment on another planet or body in space.

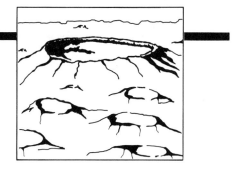

ALTERNATE QUESTIONS

1. Photographic evidence from the Viking probes shows that on a sunny day on Mars the sky is salmon pink. At night, the sky is crystal clear and colored stars beam, rather than twinkle, in the heavens. Why is the Martian sky different from Earth's?

2. Terraforming on Mars is being considered by many scientists as a possible solution for the future food and space crisis caused by overpopulation on earth. The Martian atmosphere is composed of 95 percent carbon dioxide, 2.7 percent nitrogen, 1.6 percent argon, and 1.5 percent oxygen. The temperature on Mars ranges from $-10°F$ to $+150°F$ ($-23°C$ to $+65°C$). Much of the planet is covered with permafrost. Gravity on Mars is about one-third as great as the Earth's. The day lasts approximately 24 hours. Hypothesize about the types of life on Earth that could survive in such conditions. Explain the reasons for your predictions.

3. Imagine that after six months on the planet Mars, the first astronauts are preparing to return to the Earth. During their stay, they have observed no signs of life on Mars. Suddenly a black object the size of a large beach ball (3 feet or 0.91 m in diameter) with fluorescent green spots rolls over the horizon toward the landing module. As a scientist, what three questions, in order, would give you the most important scientific information about the object? Under what circumstances would you attempt to capture the object and return to Earth with it?

4. The following headline appeared in *The New York Times* on August 27, 1911: "MARTIANS BUILD TWO IMMENSE CANALS IN TWO YEARS—Vast Engineering Works Accomplished in an Incredibly Short Time by Our Planetary Neighbors." How did the reporters and editors of one of the nation's most reliable newspapers make such an error?

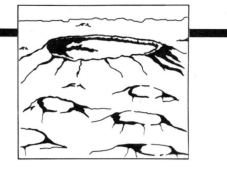

CHALLENGE: Mars or Bust!

Deciding where to land the first manned flight to Mars is probably the single most important decision for the success of a mission to Mars. Aerospace scientists will make that decision after carefully considering all of the evidence that supports various landing sites. What factors might influence their decision? Use the segment of the map of Mars, the key shown below, and library research to select a site for a landing. Explain the scientific reasons for your choice.

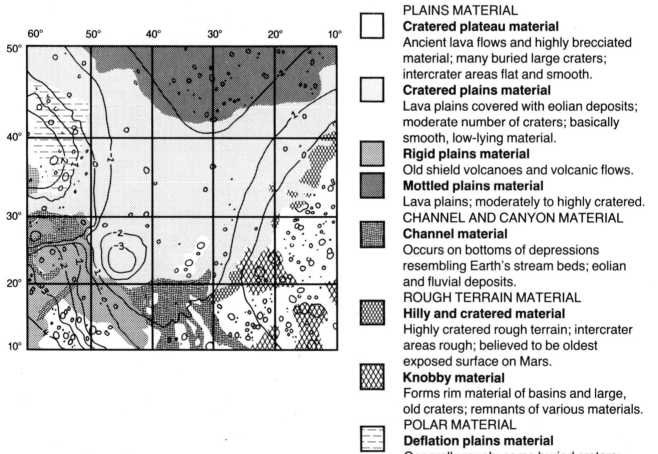

PLAINS MATERIAL
Cratered plateau material
Ancient lava flows and highly brecciated material; many buried large craters; intercrater areas flat and smooth.

Cratered plains material
Lava plains covered with eolian deposits; moderate number of craters; basically smooth, low-lying material.

Rigid plains material
Old shield volcanoes and volcanic flows.

Mottled plains material
Lava plains; moderately to highly cratered.

CHANNEL AND CANYON MATERIAL
Channel material
Occurs on bottoms of depressions resembling Earth's stream beds; eolian and fluvial deposits.

ROUGH TERRAIN MATERIAL
Hilly and cratered material
Highly cratered rough terrain; intercrater areas rough; believed to be oldest exposed surface on Mars.

Knobby material
Forms rim material of basins and large, old craters; remnants of various materials.

POLAR MATERIAL
Deflation plains material
Generally rough; some buried craters; older surface eroded by wind; relatively soft material.

15. GETTING IN SHAPE

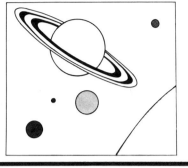

INTRODUCTION

Some phenomena are so common that we fail to notice the interesting scientific questions that they pose. In this question of the week, students investigate the standard spherical shape of bodies in the universe. This can lead to important discoveries about how matter behaves in space. The alternate questions focus on the hypotheses that human beings used long ago to explain the earth's shape. Scientific problem-solving skills are developed as students use mathematics to determine the relative smoothness of two spheres—a tennis ball and the earth condensed to the size of a tennis ball. In the challenge activity, students are asked to consider the idea that the spinning earth is a perpetual motion machine and then debate the scientific validity of various machines purported to generate more energy than they use.

QUESTION OF THE WEEK

Why are planets, moons, and suns all basically spheres instead of cubes or cylinders? What hypotheses would explain the standard shape?

Explanation

For any given mass, a sphere is the shape that has the smallest volume and surface area. The gravitational forces at work in large molten or gaseous bodies such as planets or suns tend to pull material toward the core, leaving the minimum possible matter on the surface of the body. Since the force of gravity acts fairly equally on all parts of the object, planets are basically spherical. Theories about the formation of the universe account for the forces that resulted in the formation of planets, solar systems, and galaxies.

Points to Consider

Restating the question is one good problem-solving technique that students should employ frequently. For this question, that strategy could be particularly helpful. The question might be restated as, "If planets, moons, and suns were not spheres, what shape would they be?" Encourage students to think of the advantages of various shapes in nature. The process of trying to visualize the origin and development of a cube-shaped planet, for example, would lead students to the realization that a sphere is the only shape with properties that would hold it in place in solar systems and galaxies. Cubes, cylinders, and pyramids are shapes that do not rotate steadily on an axis. As planets they would not remain in orbit but would crash into the sun or wander on erratic tracks through space.

Many objects in the universe share a standard shape. Planets and moons are roughly spherical in shape. Their elliptical orbits appear circular. Stars are spheres of hot gases. Solar systems are "round." While galaxies have a variety of shapes, in general they are spiraling circles or ovals with spiral arms. There are even some spherical galaxies. This standard shape provides physicists and astronomers with some clues about the universe and how it began. The current popular theory, called the Big Bang Theory, suggests that in the beginning superheated gases exploded with a bang. The hot gases expanded outward from the point of the explosion. After about 500 million years, the gases cooled. The cooled gases formed separate galaxies, "clouds" of atomic and subatomic particles. After about 10,000 million years more had elapsed, the particles in the gases condensed to form simple elements and eventually suns and planets.

ALTERNATE QUESTIONS

1. If the earth could be condensed to the size of a tennis ball, which ball's surface would be smoother—the earth's or the tennis ball's? Scientists constantly use mathematics as a tool to help them answer scientific questions. How could you use mathematics to answer this question? (Hint: Try fractions or ratios.)

First, estimate the diameter of the earth and the height of its surface. (Use high mountains to determine the surface height.) The diameter of the earth is close to 7000 miles (11,200 km) across. Mt. Everest, the highest mountain on earth, is about 6 miles (9.6 km) high. Then estimate the diameter of the tennis ball and the height of its surface fuzz. The diameter of a tennis ball is about 3 inches (7.6 cm). The fuzz on a tennis ball is about 1/8 inch, or 0.125 inch (0.32 cm) high. Ask students which fraction is smaller, 6/7000 or .125/3 (9.6/11,200 or 0.32/7.6)? The answer is 6/7000 (9.6/11,200). Therefore, if the earth and a tennis ball were the same size, the surface of the earth would be much smoother.

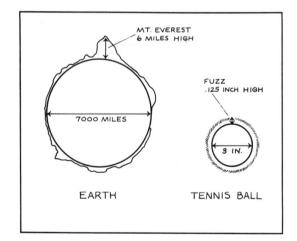

2. Even very young children ask questions such as "Why is the sun round?" or "If the earth is spinning, why can't we feel it?" Sometimes adults answer "Just because," or "You'll understand when you are older." Actually, young children can understand very complex ideas if they are explained in simple terms. Suppose a six or seven year old asked you, "Why are craters round?" Describe how you could help the child understand the answer. Then write an explanation that could be used in a second-grade science book. You may use illustrations. If possible, try out your explanation on a younger brother or sister or a young neighbor.

Answer will vary. Some students may use an example, such as ripples in a pond, to explain why craters are round. Others may explain the round shape by using a rock and soft wet earth as a model to demonstrate what happens when a rock crashes into a solid, relatively soft object. The written explanation might go something like this:

Why Craters on the Moon Are Round

A crater is a hollow area on a moon or planet. It looks like the inside of a bowl.

Craters form when rocks from space crash into the moon.

These rocks are called *meteors*.

The crashing meteors push moon rocks out of the way.

This makes a crater.

It is round because moon rocks are pushed up all around the rock.

You can make your own crater. Just drop a rock into wet sand or soft, wet earth.

3. Why can't we sense that the earth is moving, even if it is spinning at about 1000 miles (1600 km) per hour at the equator? How can airplanes take off in one place and fly to another without getting lost? Wouldn't the earth rotating beneath them cause the pilots to be about 1000 miles (1600 km) off course every hour?

Why don't we feel the earth spinning?—In order to answer this question, students must understand how human beings sense motion. The eyes and the inner ears are the major sensory organs for detecting our own movement and the movement of things around us. The eyes detect motion when images of objects move across the retina—the nervous tissue at the back of the eye. This occurs under two different conditions: (1) When we move past stationary objects.

(2) When objects around us move while we remain stationary.

The brain uses sensory information from the eyes and inner ear to help tell the difference between these two conditions. One way we know when we are moving (Condition 1) is that our inner ear has special sensory organs collectively called the *otolith* that can detect even small movements of the head. (The otolith detects acceleration, deceleration, and changes in direction.) However, once we are moving and our rate and direction remain fairly constant, we rely on our eyes and other sensory experiences, such as air pushing against our skin, to tell us we are moving. When particular objects move and we remain stationary (Condition 2), the inner ear tells us we are stationary. We see the objects move past us and also past other nearby stationary objects that are behind or in front of them.

Without any of these sensory clues, we are unable to detect any movement, regardless of how fast we are moving. In fact, there are often times when we are moving at high speeds and do not detect it. For example, on a smooth airplane ride traveling 400 miles (640 km) per hour, we don't sense any movement at all if we close our eyes. We do not detect the spinning of the earth or its movement through space because none of the necessary conditions for detecting motion are present. All the earthly objects around us are moving at the same rate we are moving. Since we are traveling at a fixed speed of about 1000 miles (1600 km) per hour, our inner ear gives us no clues about our own body's motion. The sun, moon, and stars are too far away to use as objects for comparison.

If a plane could escape the earth's atmosphere and gravity as a rocket does, then the earth would rotate from under the plane. Since the earth's atmosphere and everything in it (including the plane) rotate at 1000 miles (1600 km) per hour, there is no chance of the earth rotating 1000 miles (1600 km) beneath the plane.

4. What are some hypotheses that people proposed long ago to explain the earth's shape? Who finally figured out that the earth is round? What evidence supported this hypothesis?

Answers will vary. Two thousand years ago, Babylonians thought that the earth was a flat disk. In 900 B.C., Homer described the earth as a convex disk, or an upside down bowl. At that same time others believed that the earth was a circular plate supported by four elephants standing on a sea turtle. The Greek philosopher Anaximander of Miletus (611–546 B.C.) thought the earth was a cylinder that was curved from north to south. He believed people lived on the surface of the cylinder. Greek scholars around 350 B.C. decided that the earth must be round. Pythagoras pointed out that since the moon and sun are round, it followed that the earth must also be round. However, the theory of the flat earth persisted until the 16th century. During the 16th century the shadow of the earth during an eclipse, the disappearance of objects on the horizon, and the appearance of new constellations as one traveled south were all offered as evidence that the earth is round.

CHALLENGE: Wheels of Fortune

An inventor who could patent a machine that does more work than is required to run it would be a billionaire. The applications for such a machine are endless. Most physicists argue that perpetual motion machines are impossible given the time-tested laws of thermodynamics, which state that energy is neither created nor destroyed, and that some energy is irretrievably lost when it is converted from one form to the other. Forces like friction and electrical resistance always remove some energy from a system. Even the earth is not a perpetual motion machine. Although it has been spinning for billions of years, it is slowing down each year. Scientists believe that during the period when dinosaurs roamed the earth, the day was about 26 hours long.

Each of the machines in the diagram also uses more energy than it produces and will thus eventually stop. The overbalanced wheel was first proposed by the inventor Villard de Honnecourt, a 13th century architect. He believed that the energy extracted from the falling weights on one side of the wheel was greater than the energy required to raise them up the other side. He reasoned that the weights would deliver more effort if they were further removed from the center of rotation. The closed-cycle water mill was designed in 1618 by English physician Robert Fludd. He reasoned that if the water that turns a mill could be collected and returned to the reservoir above the wheel, then the need for a source of running water would be eliminated. He designed a pump run by the water wheel that is able to do this. The inventor believed falling water produced more energy than was required to return the water to the reservoir. The fact that these machines worked in theory only (after hundreds of tries no one could ever get one to work) should have been strong evidence that the original hypothesis was probably wrong.

CHALLENGE TERMS

- **oblate** Flattened at the poles. The earth is an oblate spheroid body.
- **otolith** The organs of a human being's inner ear that are responsible for detecting acceleration, deceleration, and changes in direction.
- **perpetual motion** The continuous operation of a device, or movement of an object, that produces more energy than it uses.
- **1st Law of Thermodynamics** Includes the Law of Conservation of Energy, which states that energy can be transformed into another form of energy but not destroyed.
- **2nd Law of Thermodynamics** States that heat cannot pass from a colder body to a hotter body without work being done.

QUESTION OF THE WEEK

Why are planets, moons, and suns all basically spheres instead of cubes or cylinders? What hypotheses would explain the standard shape?

115

GLOSSARY

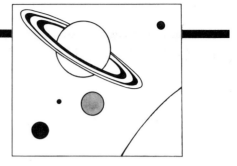

circumference   The perimeter of a circle, the length of the line that makes a circle, or the length of a line around a sphere at its equator.

diameter   The length of a line segment that passes through the center of a circle, whose end points lie on the circle.

proportion   Some part of a whole object, stated as a fraction or percent. When the measurements of one object are a constant fraction of the measurements of another, we say the objects are proportional.

radius   The length of a line segment that joins the center of a circle and a point on the circle. The radius of a circle is always equal to 1/2 of its diameter.

ratio   The mathematical relationship, stated as a fraction or percent, between the quantity, amount, or size of two things. For example, the ratio of the earth's volume to the sun's is about 1 to 1,300,000. This means it would take 1,300,000 earths to equal one sun.

revolution   The motion of a planet or moon moving around the sun or another planet. For instance, the moon revolves around the earth and the earth revolves around the sun.

rotation   The process of turning, or spinning, about an axis. The earth makes one complete rotation about its axis every 24 hours. It spins at about 1000 miles (1600 km) per hour at the equator.

sensory information   Information that we get from our five senses: touch, sound, sight, taste, and smell.

spheroid   An object having the shape of a ball or globe.

spiral galaxy   A huge rotating star system that has a "disk" of stars in its center and long "arms" of stars, gases, and dust curving off of the disk. The Milky Way, earth's galaxy, is an example of a spiral galaxy.

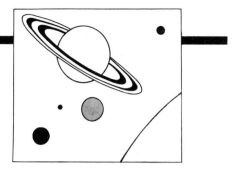

ALTERNATE QUESTIONS

1. If the earth could be condensed to the size of a tennis ball, which ball's surface would be smoother—the earth's or the tennis ball's? Scientists constantly use mathematics as a tool to help them answer scientific questions. How could you use mathematics to answer this question? (Hint: Try fractions or ratios.)

2. Even very young children ask questions such as "Why is the sun round?" or "If the earth is spinning why can't we feel it?" Sometimes adults answer "Just because," or "You'll understand when you are older." Actually, young children can understand very complex ideas if they are explained in simple terms. Suppose a six or seven year old asked you, "Why are craters round?" Describe how you could help the child understand the answer. Then write an explanation that could be used in a second-grade science book. You may use illustrations. If possible, try out your explanation on a younger brother or sister or a young neighbor.

3. Why can't we sense that the earth is moving, even if it is spinning at about 1000 miles (1600 km) per hour at the equator? How can airplanes take off in one place and fly to another without getting lost? Wouldn't the earth rotating beneath them cause the pilots to be about 1000 miles (1600 km) off course every hour?

4. What are some hypotheses that people long ago proposed to explain the earth's shape? Who finally figured out that the earth is round? What evidence supported that hypothesis?

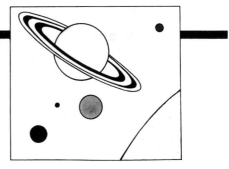

CHALLENGE: Wheels of Fortune

Debate about the concept of perpetual motion has gone on for centuries. In simple terms, supporters believe that once a perpetual motion machine or device is started, it can continue indefinitely without any additional energy from outside sources. Other people argue that the laws of physics demonstrate that such a machine cannot be produced.

Inventors are often among the strongest supporters of such a machine. Over one hundred years ago one inventor claimed to have scientific proof that perpetual motion machines could exist. "You are standing on one," he claimed. "The round earth spinning under your feet is a perpetual motion machine. It was set in motion by God and will continue for all of eternity." More recently, Mr. Joseph Newman of Lucedale, Mississippi, claims to have invented and tested a machine that is 800 percent efficient. This means the machine produces about eight times more energy than it uses. A few engineers and physicists have signed a statement saying that they believe Mr. Newman's claims are true. Most say he needs a day in a laboratory where he can have the machine tested under controlled conditions. He is trying to convince the U.S. Patent Office to grant him a patent on his perpetual motion machine.

Why are inventors so interested in patenting a perpetual motion machine? What scientific laws do opponents use to refute the inventors' claims? The earth has been spinning for about 4.5 billion years. In your opinion, does the spinning earth qualify as a perpetual motion machine? Support your opinion with scientific evidence.

Analyze each of the designs for perpetual motion machines shown. Describe how each one is supposed to work. Would you submit either of these devices for a patent? Write a letter to each inventor stating your position on the design. State your opinion in scientific terms.

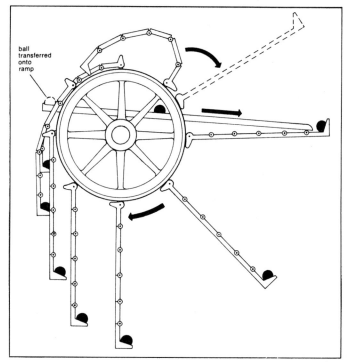

ball
transferred
onto
ramp

Typical overbalanced wheel

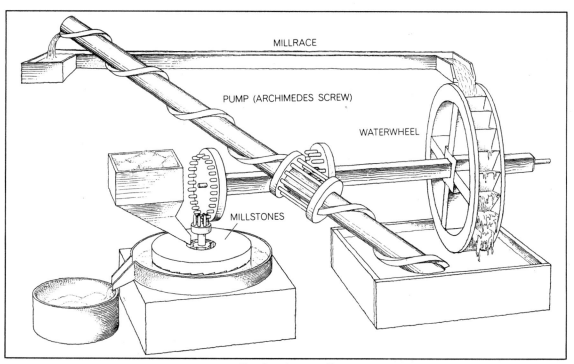

MILLRACE

PUMP (ARCHIMEDES SCREW)

WATERWHEEL

MILLSTONES

Closed-cycle water mill.

16. DON'T TAKE IT FOR GRANITE! Aerospace Science

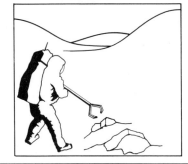

INTRODUCTION

Sometimes a simple piece of evidence, such as a rock, contains a surprising amount of information when it is carefully examined by a scientist. In this unit, students must infer the geological history of the moon from the composition of moon rocks. They will discover how current geological features on the moon can be used as evidence to make inferences about the rest of our solar system and about events that occurred millions of years ago on earth. Scientific ingenuity is encouraged as students are challenged to describe all of the scientific information they could gather about the moon using only a few hand tools and the keen observational skills of a scientist.

QUESTION OF THE WEEK

How do rocks that astronauts gathered on the moon's surface compare with rocks and minerals on earth? How did geologists' discoveries change how we view the moon?

Explanation

Apollo astronauts collected over 2000 samples from six different lunar sites. Since the surface of the moon is unprotected by atmosphere and unaffected by erosion, moon rocks offer an uninterrupted record of all the events that have occurred since the formation of our solar system. Geologists have found rocks from the moon that are 4600 million years old, while the oldest earth rocks found to date are only 3800 million years old.

Most of the rocks are similar to those found on earth. Three examples of earthly types are basalt found in the moon's "Sea of Tranquillity" and aluminum and titanium found in the lunar highlands. However, the proportions of elements in the lunar rocks differs from that of earth. For instance, the moon has less iron and fewer volatile elements (those that vaporize easily) but more of the involatile elements such as aluminum, calcium, and uranium. In addition to these differences, geologists were surprised to find three new minerals (armalcolite, pyroxferroite, and tranquillityite) that have never been found on the earth. Armalcolite was named for Apollo 11 astronauts Armstrong, Aldrin, and Collins. Pyroxferroite is a combination of pyroxine and iron (pyrox plus ferroite). Tranquillityite was named for the site where it was discovered, at Tranquillity Base in the Sea of Tranquillity.

Prior to the Apollo landings, it was thought that the moon's surface might consist of primitive planetary material. However, all the lunar samples are products of igneous processes in which molten material solidifies and fragments repeatedly as meteors strike the moon's surface. This discovery changed geologists' views on the moon's origins, supporting the theory that the moon developed separately from the earth. Another theory about the moon's origin, that it was once a part of the earth that broke away and was then captured in orbit around it, now seems much less likely.

Points to Consider

When NASA geologists first examined the moon rocks, they compared them to a bag of charcoal. They appeared unimpressive and were covered with a grey, powdery, gritty substance. Astronauts often complained about having to gather the rocks since the powder rubbed off on their suits. The moon rock in the poster was collected by the crew of the Apollo 12 mission. This microscopic view of a paper-thin section of the rock shows relatively large crystals, about 1 mm across. These large crystals are porphyritic, a term derived from the Greek work *porphyros* for purple. A porphyry is any igneous rock with large, distinct crystals. The large crystals are the mineral olivine. The others are pyroxenes, feldspars, and metal compounds. The texture and mineralogy of the moon rocks are common in volcanic rocks on earth.

ALTERNATE QUESTIONS

1. What are some theories that have been proposed to explain the origin of the earth's moon? How have moon rocks changed geologists' theories about the origin of the moon?

The origin and development of the moon is a mystery that has intrigued astronomers for centuries. The moon is just over a quarter of the earth's size; it is larger relative to its parent planet than the satellites of any other planet in the solar system. In fact, some astronomers refer to the earth and the moon as a "double planet." While the earth and the moon probably formed at about the same time, there has been much scientific debate about whether they formed together or separately.

At least three major hypotheses have been proposed to explain the origin of the moon:
1. The moon was once a part of the earth that broke away and was then captured by the earth's gravity. A more modern version of this hypothesis proposes that the earth and Mars were once one planet that split, sending the earth into one orbit around the sun and Mars into the other. The moon, a large fragment from the explosion, was cast away with the earth and fell into orbit around it.
2. The moon formed near the earth, possibly from a ring of rocky particles that was orbiting the earth. It remained in orbit after forming.
3. The moon formed somewhere else in the solar system and was then captured by the earth's

gravity. Much of the recent evidence on the moon's composition comes from the rocks gathered by the Apollo astronauts and points to this last hypothesis.

2. Scientists predict that mining operations will begin on the moon's surface before the year 2010. What advice would you have for a company that wanted to mine for coal on the moon? Why would some types of rocks and minerals be unlikely to be found on the moon's surface? Give some specific examples and discuss some possible reasons for their absence.

There is absolutely no evidence of any past or present life on the moon. This means that carbon, a very prevalent element on earth, is not present on the moon. Since coal is a carbon-based fossil fuel that forms from the bodies of dead plants and animals, it is very likely that the company would go bankrupt. Any carbon-based minerals such as diamonds would also not be found. Sedimentary rocks such as limestone and sandstone, which are formed by erosive forces on the earth's surface, are not present in their true form on the moon's surface.

3. Using a polarizing light, geologists have discovered that moon rocks are solid jumbles of many kinds of rock crystals. They have named these formations of igneous rocks *breccia* after a type of sedimentary rock on earth. Since there is no weathering process on the moon to form sedimentary rocks, what physical forces on the moon might account for the formation of breccia?

In order to form a hypothesis about the formation of breccia, students must understand the forces that shaped the moon's surface billions of years ago. During its first 700 million years we know that the moon was pelted by meteors that hit and melted its hard lava surface, creating large craters. We know the impact of these meteors cast rocks over wide areas of the moon's surface. Geologists believe that as centuries went by, these fragments became welded together and broken apart many times from countless meteor showers. This process was probably responsible for the breccia on the moon's surface.

4. The "Sea of Tranquillity" (Mare Tranquillitatis) and the "Sea of Showers" (Mare Imbrium) are features on the moon that were named by Galileo and other early astronomers. They believed these dark flat areas, called *maria*, were oceans. If the moon never had water, what caused the moon's maria? If liquid water had existed on the moon at one time, how would geologists know?

Scientists believe that about 3.9 billion years ago heat generated by radioactivity accumulated inside the moon. This intense heat melted a layer of rock several hundred kilometers beneath the moon's surface. About 3.5 billion years ago, as large meteors fractured the moon's surface, the dark molten rock flowed up through the cracks, creating the vast lava plains called maria. Although the moon does not show the mountain-building volcanic activity of earth, rock samples gathered from these areas are basaltic lavas similar to those found on earth. If liquid water had existed on the moon in the past, geologists might expect to see signs of sedimentation and erosion of rocks in ancient lakes or stream beds.

CHALLENGE: Technical Difficulties

Answers will vary. Sample responses: You could see weathering or lack of weathering; number, size, and condition of surface features such as craters and mountains; presence or absence of faults, active volcanoes, and unusual features such as rilles and maria; presence or absence of surface water and atmosphere; relative age of rock formations; presence or absence of crystals in rocks. By carefully examining rock samples, you could determine their sizes, shapes, colors, and surface textures (smooth or rough). You could classify various rocks as igneous, metamorphic, or sedimentary based on features you could see. The pick and shovel would allow you to dig for samples beneath the surface dust. These tools could then be used to break rocks apart and to test rocks for hardness, relative density, and fracture or cleavage (breaking along a plane surface parallel to a crystal). The hand compass could detect the presence or absence of lodestones, providing a clue to the magnetic field of moon.

CHALLENGE TERMS

- **rilles**   Long, winding trenches that are found near the edges of maria and inside large craters on the moon.
- **terrae**   The very bright surfaces that appear on two-thirds of the moon's surface. Terrae are caused by light reflecting off the rugged highlands.
- **maria**   The latin word for "oceans." The name *maria* was given to the large, flat plains on the moon by early observers who believed that the moon had oceans like the earth. From earth, the maria appear dark because they absorb rather than reflect much of the sun's light.
- **porphyry**   A rock consisting of feldspar crystals embedded in a compact dark-red aggregate of stone. The term also refers to any igneous rock with the same texture.
- **regolith**   The 30-foot layer of fine packed dust that covers the moon's surface. The layer was created by the sandblasting effect of numerous meteorites and micrometeorites.

QUESTION OF THE WEEK

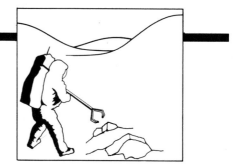

How do rocks that astronauts gathered on the moon's surface compare with rocks and minerals on earth? How did geologists' discoveries change how we view the moon?

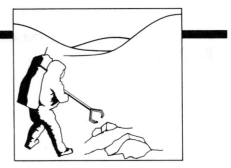

GLOSSARY

aggregate   Composed of mineral crystals of one or more kinds of mineral rock fragments.

basalt   A dark grey or black igneous rock that is formed when magma (molten rock) from within a volcano erupts as lava and then hardens.

breccia   Sedimentary rocks consisting of sharp fragments embedded in a sandstone-like base. The fragments can be igneous, sedimentary, or metamorphic rocks.

feldspar   The most abundant mineral on earth. Rocks in the feldspar group are found in igneous, metamorphic, and sedimentary rocks.

igneous rocks   Rocks that are formed by the cooling and hardening of molten rock material.

metamorphic rocks   Rocks that are formed through the alteration of igneous and sedimentary rocks by heat and pressure.

polarized light   Light in which all waves are vibrating in a single plane. Light waves can be polarized by shining a light source through a filter that allows only certain wavelengths to pass through. The rest are reflected or absorbed. There is more contrast in colors seen through a polarizing filter.

sedimentary rocks   Rocks that are produced by the accumulation of rock waste (called sediment) at the earth's surface.

tungsten   A grey and white metallic element often found in quartz veins. Tungsten is valued for its use in hardening steel.

volatile elements   Elements that readily change into vapor at relatively low temperatures.

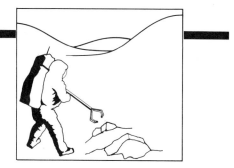

ALTERNATE QUESTIONS

1. What are some theories that have been proposed to explain the origin of the earth's moon? How have moon rocks changed geologists' theories about the origin of the moon?

2. Scientists predict that mining operations will begin on the moon's surface before the year 2010. What advice would you have for a company that wanted to mine for coal on the moon? Why would some types of rocks and minerals be unlikely to be found on the moon's surface? Give some specific examples and discuss some possible reasons for their absence.

3. Using a polarizing light, geologists have discovered that moon rocks are solid jumbles of many kinds of rock crystals. They have named these formations of igneous rocks *breccia* after a type of sedimentary rock on earth. Since there is no weathering process on the moon to form sedimentary rocks, what physical forces on the moon might account for the formation of breccia?

4. The "Sea of Tranquillity" (Mare Tranquillitatis) and the "Sea of Showers" (Mare Imbrium) are features on the moon that were named by Galileo and other early astronomers. They believed these dark flat areas, called *maria*, were oceans. If the moon never had water, what caused the moon's maria? If liquid water had existed on the moon at one time, how would geologists know?

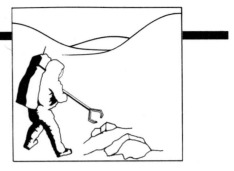

CHALLENGE: Technical Difficulties

Apollo astronauts who walked on the moon spent many months studying geology. NASA wanted these astronauts to be able to look at the moon's surface through the eyes of a geologist as they collected rock and soil samples. They were trained to observe and carefully describe the moon in geological terms. Just in case their instruments failed or they were unable to bring back extremely large samples, they were even trained to perform geological tests without any special technical equipment. As one astronaut remarked, "I felt like a space age prospector from a 19th century gold rush."

How many things could you learn about the moon, its rocks, and its geology with sharp eyes, a keen mind, and a few basic hand tools such as a pick, hammer, shovel, and compass? Identify fifty facts or ideas.